LILLY fOR COMPANY

Austin Casual Menus
for Palm & Plate

by Jane Lilly Schotz

Enjoy!
Jane Lilly Schotz

Photography by Weston Giunta
Design by Liz Tindall

Lilly for Company:
Austin Casual Menus for Palm and Plate

Inquiries should be addressed to:

Culinaria
Jane Lilly Schotz
P. O. Box 5902
Austin, TX 78763-5902

To order books, call 512-689-3246.

First Printing 2004

Cataloging-in Publication Data

Schotz, Jane Lilly

Lilly for Company: Austin Casual Menus for Palm and Plate

p.   cm.   illus.

1. Entertaining. 2. Dinners and dining. 3. Cookery. 4. Menus. 5. Caterers and Catering--Texas

I. Title. II. Author. III. Monograph. IV. Photos

ISBN 0-9763519-0-0

641.5 S9451   TX 731 S28 2004

Printed in Austin, Texas, USA

For Max and Mai

Table of Contents

I started Lilly & Co. because I wanted to cook all day in a small environment with people I liked. In 1984, I found a sweet old house in Austin's historic Clarksville neighborhood, and opened shop with a limited menu and very limited staff. As the business grew, I hired people based on interviews that revealed their favorite movies and the books they were reading. I knew that to spend countless hours together in a small and hot kitchen we needed a good mix. I was lucky to hire many employees who are still dear friends. I learned at least a little, often a lot, from each person who worked with me. The recipes in this book were created, adapted, improved, and tested by us all.

I owe a debt of gratitude to these Lilly alumni, especially to those who stayed a while. Their different perspectives, creativity, energy, and hard work were essential in the development of the recipes in this book. The names are too many to list—and I would no doubt make terrible omissions—but they know who they are.

I am also grateful to our loyal customers for their copious feedback and support. My family and friends did more than their share, too, from landscaping the shop yard to helping me celebrate retirement, answering a few desperate calls in between.

I appreciate everyone's contribution, from the Lilly's early days until fourteen years later, when I closed the shop to spend more time with my family.

Thanks to you all.

Thanks also to:
Weston Giunta, for his meticulous work to produce gorgeous photographs.

Ronna Welsh, for her thorough and attentive editing, for keeping my voice and remembering the food.

Liz Tindall, for the lovely design.

ABOUT THIS BOOK

I was always stumped that recipes and caterers' menu items claimed, without context, to feed a certain number of people. I wondered, were they big people or little people? Were they at a quick meeting or wandering a party into the late hours? Were there other food items on their table? Were they eating before dinner, at dinnertime, after dinner, or late at night?

When a catering customer called "The Lilly," I asked him a lot of questions before I could offer him menus. I couldn't recommend a fork and knife meal, for example, if the host didn't have tables to set for guests. If a client was having a party 45 minutes from town, he needed substantial food to entice his friends to stick around. If he didn't have kitchen help, he couldn't consider something that required a lot of last-minute attention. I wouldn't recommend 10 dishes for 20 guests at a cocktail hour and I certainly wouldn't suggest 3 items that would require a last minute deep fry. And if he had a small oven and no plans to rent chafer pans, he couldn't serve a warm menu to a large crowd.

This book presents a series of menus for different gatherings. I've divided the book into sections that suit different serving styles: there are finger menus, fork menus, fork and knife menus, and soups. Most of the dishes can be prepared ahead of time to a certain point because I know that it's work enough to ready the house and stage a meal, even one that requires minimal attention. There's enough to manage—water glasses to fill, bread to warm, wine to chill, and guests to greet—without adding further complications. The point of entertaining is to have fun. A relaxed host is a better host. Friends of mine might argue that I have taken this platform to extremes, emerging from a long bath at the sound of my husband greeting our first guests. But I join the party relaxed and happy, and hope you do so as well.

Enjoy.

My style of cooking uses as many fresh ingredients as possible. While there is beauty in the fresh item, there is also inconsistency. It's where art meets cooking. Two pounds of tomatoes one week will not be just like two pounds of tomatoes the next. One hot pepper might not even wake up your taste buds and another could make you cry.

Therefore, you have to taste as you cook. Taste how table salt compares to kosher salt and sea salt. Taste a cold soup after it has chilled—the warm soup is a different animal. Taste a salad dressing with a carrot to see how it will taste when it's served.

Choose the salt, balsamic vinegar, chocolate, olive oil, canned tomato, etc. that suits your palate. Think about what you're looking for and what ingredient will take you there.

Adding sugar for balance:
Some recipes, in particular ones with tomatoes and dried chiles, might taste slightly flat or tinny. A tiny bit of sugar will often work magic to bring the dish back into balance and brighten flavors.

Roasting peppers:
To roast a pepper, place directly on a gas stovetop flame or under a broiler. Turn the pepper until it is evenly blackened and blistered. Cool in a paper bag to steam the pepper and loosen the skin. Rub the skin off under running water. It's a good idea to wear rubber or latex gloves when handling the hot peppers, as they will irritate the skin.

Basil Purée:
I keep puréed fresh basil in olive oil in my freezer all year. To prepare it, combine 1 cup of packed leaves, washed and dried well, with ⅓ cup olive oil in a processor bowl fitted with a metal blade. Process until finely chopped, adding more olive oil if necessary. It will keep for months in the freezer. The equivalent of 2 tablespoons of purée is about ⅓ cup packed fresh leaves, chopped. Though I give measurements in the recipes, I don't think there is such a thing as too much fresh basil and I recommend using it to taste.

Checking custards for doneness:
I went to cooking school in England, where custards are taken seriously and are usually silky and light in texture. The cooking times of these custards are a little tricky to predict. I've made hundreds of them over the years and have found that there is no consistent formula for cooking time; that the same recipe made in the same oven at the same temperature will sometimes take much longer or less time than another batch. The timing does depend on the oven and the size of the dish (and, perhaps, how the planets align). You just have to check them. They should wobble like something made with gelatin—not totally stiff, not liquid—when you tap the side of the cooking cup. Since my home oven is hopelessly slow, I often remove the cover for the last few minutes of cooking. It gives them a little direct heat boost, but doesn't expose them long enough to make them form a thick skin on top. Also note that convection heat doesn't work well for the dessert custards in this book, but is fine for quiche and corn timbale.

fINGER fOOD

CASUAL COCKTAIL BUFFET FOR 40

CHICKEN BREASTS STUFFED WITH APPLES AND WALNUTS
PEPPER CHEESE SPREAD
ASPARAGUS WITH SPICY PEANUT DIP
WILD MUSHROOM POLENTA TRIANGLES

This menu is nice and light. If you think that your guests will make dinner of the buffet, you might want to add corn tarts (page 19), more vegetables, or maybe even a roasted beef tenderloin (with rolls or bread to keep it finger-friendly). The chicken breasts also make a nice entrée for dinner. Overall, the menu is low maintenance — each item is good at room temperature and requires little last minute fuss

CHICKEN BREASTS STUFFED WITH APPLES AND WALNUTS

2 tablespoons butter
1 large yellow onion, chopped fine
2 cloves garlic, minced
3 Granny Smith apples, peeled and cut into small cubes
1 pear, peeled and cut into small cubes
1¾ cups toasted walnut pieces
2 ounces fresh goat cheese (chevre), room temperature
¼ cup cream cheese, room temperature
1 teaspoon dried sage leaves
¼ cup currants
1 tablespoon brown sugar (more if needed)
pinch cayenne pepper
2 tablespoons brandy
kosher salt and fresh ground black pepper to taste
13 whole (26 halves) boneless skinless chicken breasts,
    4 ounces each half
4 tablespoons melted butter

In a large sauté pan over medium heat, melt the butter and add the onion and garlic and sauté 2 or 3 minutes. Add the apples and pear and cook until soft. Remove from heat and add the other stuffing ingredients, making sure that the walnuts are not hot (your stuffing will turn purple if they are). Adjust seasonings.

Cover part of your work surface with plastic wrap. Spread out several breast halves on the plastic and cover them with plastic wrap. With the smooth side of a meat mallet, pound the chicken breasts to even thickness. To fill, lay the chicken breasts out skin-side down. Spoon about 3 tablespoons of the filling across the middle of each breast. Fold the tops and bottoms of the breasts to the center to cover the filling, matching the edges to seal the stuffing inside. Place the stuffed breast halves, seam side down, in a buttered roasting pan.

Preheat oven to 375°. Season rolled breasts with salt and pepper and brush with melted butter. Bake until cooked through, about 20 minutes. When cool, slice each breast half into 4 slices. Pierce each slice with a 4-inch bamboo skewer for finger buffets. Serves about 40 for cocktails or 20 for dinner.

To serve warm as an entrée, serve with a velouté sauce: In a small saucepan over medium heat, melt 2 tablespoons of butter. Add 1 tablespoon flour and whisk for 1 minute. Whisk in the pan drippings and 1½ cups chicken stock. Bring to a boil and season with salt, pepper, and a dash of cayenne.

PEPPER CHEESE SPREAD

We used to double this recipe and mold it in a loaf pan lined with plastic wrap. It will slice nicely for serving.

1½ pounds cream cheese
4 ounces grated Cheddar cheese
4 ounces grated Monterey Jack cheese
1 poblano pepper, roasted, peeled, seeded, and chopped (see note page 9)
6 sun-dried tomato halves, softened in hot water and chopped
3 tablespoons capers
3 tablespoons chopped green olives
2 large shallots, chopped

In a mixing bowl, beat the cream cheese until soft and fluffy. Add the Cheddar and Jack cheeses and beat until well mixed and very soft. Add the rest of the ingredients and mix until just blended; over mixing with the olives and capers may curdle the mixture. For best flavor, serve at room temperature.

Makes 2 pounds, enough to serve about 30 to 40 at a cocktail hour. Keeps about 2 weeks if well wrapped.

ASPARAGUS WITH SPICY PEANUT DIP

I once heard that there were those who would judge the wealth of a host by how much of the asparagus stem she trimmed. I like to use as much of a healthy spear as is tender. Be sure to choose asparagus with firm tips (not soft and slimy) and green (not dry or woody) stems.

5 bunches (about 150 spears) thin asparagus, trimmed

12 ounces cream cheese or Neufchâtel
⅔ cup creamy peanut butter (good-quality natural)
¾ teaspoon cayenne pepper
⅓ cup rice wine vinegar
½ teaspoon black pepper
⅓ cup soy sauce, more if necessary
2 tablespoons chopped or whole peanuts for garnish

To cook asparagus, boil about 4 quarts of water in a large stockpot. Cook the asparagus spears in batches, taking care not to crowd the water, for 1½ to 2 minutes. Remove with tongs and cool in a bowl of ice water to stop the cooking and preserve the green color. Refrigerate.

For the dip, beat the cream cheese in a mixing bowl until soft and fluffy. Add the peanut butter, cayenne, vinegar, pepper, and soy sauce. Adjust seasonings to taste. Serve at room temperature. I garnish the dip with peanuts to alert those who can't eat nuts.

Makes about 2½ cups.

WILD MUSHROOM POLENTA TRIANGLES

This polenta is versatile—it can also be cut into large side servings and topped with pesto, tomato sauce, or grilled vegetables. You can prepare this recipe ahead and refrigerate it in the baking pan, before or after it is baked. *Note:* if you double the recipe, cook only one recipe of the polenta in the saucepan at a time (with the weight of a double batch, it will scorch too easily).

½ cup fresh or dried wild mushrooms (morels or mixed)
2 tablespoons butter
3 medium shallots, chopped
1½ cups chopped white mushrooms or cremini
2 tablespoons sherry
1½ cups water
4½ cups milk
1½ teaspoons kosher salt
fresh ground black pepper
6 tablespoons unsalted butter, cut small
1½ cups quick polenta (if not using quick, follow cooking
    times on package)
1 cup grated Parmesan, plus more to sprinkle triangles
2 eggs, lightly beaten

Butter a 9 X 13 X 2-inch pan and line the bottom with waxed paper. If using dried wild mushrooms, pour hot water over them in a bowl. Let them sit for 5 minutes. Strain and rinse well. In a small sauté pan, melt the butter and add the shallots, both kinds of mushrooms, and sherry. Cook over medium heat until soft. Set aside.

Preheat oven to 350°. In a large saucepan, combine the water, milk, salt, pepper, and butter and stir over medium heat. When the butter has melted, whisk in the polenta a little at a time. Add the mushroom mixture and stir continuously over medium heat until the mixture thickens (about 10 minutes), scraping the bottom and sides of the pan to prevent sticking. Remove from heat and let the mixture sit for about 10 minutes before thoroughly mixing in the eggs and Parmesan and pouring it into the prepared pan. Smooth the top with a spatula or buttered fingers. Bake until the top begins to brown, for 20 to 30 minutes. Cool before cutting.

To cut, run a knife around the edge of the pan. Cover with a cutting board and gently invert. Lift off the pan, remove the waxed paper and cut the rectangle into 24 (2-inch) squares. Cut the squares into triangles and transfer to a greased cookie sheet, spaced about 1 inch apart. Sprinkle with Parmesan and bake at 350° for 7 or 8 minutes, until slightly crisp. Serve warm or at room temperature.

Makes 4 dozen small triangles or 12 to 16 side servings.

COCKTAIL BUFFET FOR 30

BLUE CRABMEAT AND CHIPOTLE CHEESECAKE
AVOCADO AND PEACH PICO DE GALLO
SESAME-GINGER CHICKEN SKEWERS
CORN TARTS

You can prepare this entire menu up to a day in advance. Just add the avocado to the pico de gallo at the last minute.

Should you want to bulk up the table a little, add steamed vegetables with a dip or fresh cut fruit. With the cheesecake, you will need 3 or 4 boxes of crackers. For the pico, you will need about 2 pounds of tortilla chips, sturdy ones for dipping.

BLUE CRABMEAT AND CHIPOTLE CHEESECAKE

If blue crabmeat is unavailable, Dungeness will work just as well in this recipe. I prefer the claw meat of the blue crab; its flavor is sweeter and more intense than the popular lump and back fin meats, and it is less expensive.

I have had great success with this cheesecake using a 10-inch, straight-sided cake pan. If you are the nervous sort, or prone to kitchen disaster, use a springform pan instead. In either case, aluminum or non-stick is better than steel, which may leave behind a not-so-tasty rust after prolonged use. To prepare the pan, brush the bottom and side well with butter then line the bottom with waxed paper. Butter the top of the waxed paper as well. If you are not using a springform, prepare the side of the pan with buttered paper too.

For the crust:
1 cup finely ground French bread crumbs (made with lightly toasted, day-old French bread)
3 tablespoons butter

For the cheesecake:
2 pounds cream cheese or Neufchâtel, room temperature
1 tablespoon butter
½ cup finely chopped red onion
½ cup finely chopped red bell pepper
8 ounces sour cream (low fat is fine)
3 tablespoons chipotle peppers in adobo sauce, minced
2 tablespoons concentrated tomato paste, in tube
   (4 tablespoons canned paste)
2 teaspoons lemon juice
½ pound blue crab claw meat
½ cup grated Monterey Jack cheese
4 large eggs
1 teaspoon kosher salt
fresh ground pepper to taste

Preheat the oven to 350°. Place the breadcrumbs in the prepared pan. Tilt the pan to coat the sides well. Shake and tap the pan to distribute the crumbs on the bottom.

In a mixing bowl, whip the cream cheese until soft, scraping the bowl often. Meanwhile, sauté the onion and bell pepper in the butter over medium heat until soft. Add to the cream cheese. Mix in the rest of the ingredients, adding the eggs last and only one at a time, beating as little as possible after each addition. When mixed well, pour the batter into the prepared pan. Set the pan in a larger roasting pan and add warm water to the roasting pan until it reaches halfway up the sides of the cheesecake pan.

Bake about 1 hour, until the cheesecake has risen a little and the middle has a firm wobble. A paring knife inserted into the middle of the cake should look beaded, neither milky nor clean.

Cool at room temperature for about 45 minutes, then refrigerate for at least 2 hours before serving. To remove the cheesecake from the pan, run a knife around the outside of the cake, then unhinge the side of the spring form and carefully lift off. To remove the bottom of the pan, cover the top of the cake with plastic wrap and invert a lightweight plate on top. Holding the plate and pan bottom securely in both hands, quickly turn the cake upside down. With a knife, pry the bottom of the pan from the cheesecake. Remove the waxed paper. Center the serving platter over the bottom of the cake and flip once more.

Serve with crackers or bread. A half recipe can be made in a 6 or 7-inch pan, baked for about 45 minutes.

Serves about 30.

AVOCADO AND PEACH PICO DE GALLO

In most of the country, you want to make this only in the summer. But in Texas, we have good hothouse tomatoes and South American produce even in the winter. You can make this relish with or without avocado, and substitute ripe mangos for peaches. Serve with tortilla chips.

Use only the leaves of the cilantro—its stems taste soapy.

8 medium Roma tomatoes, chopped
1 medium yellow onion, finely chopped
2 serrano peppers, seeded and minced
juice of 4 limes
¼ cup cilantro leaves, chopped
3 avocados, chopped
3 ripe peaches, peeled (see below) and chopped
kosher salt and fresh ground black pepper to taste

You may prepare each of the ingredients ahead of time, except for the avocado, which will start to turn brown once exposed to air. Store all prepared ingredients separately and combine right before serving.

To peel peaches, drop them 1 or 2 at a time into boiling water. Remove with a slotted spoon after 1 minute. To peel, score the skin into strips and pull off with a paring knife.

Makes about 2 quarts.

SESAME-GINGER CHICKEN SKEWERS

Even my picky kids will eat these. I made them for my son's 6th birthday party and everyone devoured them with reckless abandon. They are great at room temperature.

For the marinade:
½ cup tomato paste
3 cloves of garlic, minced
2 medium shallots, peeled and cut in half
¼ cup cilantro leaves
⅓ cup rice wine vinegar
½ cup packed light brown sugar
⅓ cup toasted sesame oil
¼ cup olive oil
2 tablespoons grated fresh ginger
3 tablespoons white sugar
⅔ cup soy sauce
juice of 2 lemons

about 4 pounds boneless, skinless chicken breasts,
    trimmed of fat and sliced into ½-inch wide strips
¾ cup sesame seeds
About 60 (6-inch) wooden skewers
¼ cup chopped cilantro leaves, optional, for garnish

Combine all of the marinade ingredients in the blender and puree until smooth. Toss the chicken strips in the marinade, coating well. Cover and let sit in the refrigerator at least 3 hours or overnight.

Preheat oven to 375°. Thread the chicken onto the wooden skewers. Arrange in a single layer on a wire rack over a roasting pan or prop the ends of the skewers on the edge of the pan so that the chicken doesn't lie flat in the bottom. Sprinkle with the sesame seeds and bake for 7 to 10 minutes, until cooked through. Alternatively, you may grill the chicken, in which case the skewers should be soaked in water for 30 minutes before use. Garnish with chopped cilantro if desired. Wipe extra marinade off ends of the skewers if they are messy.

Makes 50 to 60 skewers.

This marinade also works very well with chicken quarters. One batch is enough to marinate 10 to 12 pieces.

CORN TARTS

These tarts are the offspring of Lilly & Co.'s popular corn timbale (page 53). They make a nice alternative to miniature quiches. I prefer to bake the tarts in English "jelly" pans that have shallow cups with slightly sloped sides. Be sure to spray the pans with cooking spray before use.

1 batch Short Crust Pastry, page 30

For the filling:
3 eggs, lightly beaten
3 ears of fresh corn, stripped of silks, rinsed and cut
    from cobs
1 teaspoon salt
½ teaspoon pepper
dash Tabasco sauce
3 tablespoons sugar
2 tablespoons chopped cilantro leaves
½ cup grated Monterey Jack cheese
1½ cups heavy cream
1 poblano pepper, roasted (see note page 9), seeded, peeled,
    & chopped

For the topping:
⅓ cup fresh goat cheese, crumbled
fresh ground black pepper

Roll the pastry to about ⅛-inch thickness. Cut into 48 rounds to fit baking pans and gently press into tart forms. Prick each with a fork and chill for about 20 minutes.

Preheat oven to 375°. In a medium bowl, combine all the filling ingredients. Carefully fill chilled tart shells. Top with goat cheese and pepper. Bake uncovered for 12 to 15 minutes, until the pastry turns golden brown and the filling puffs up. If not serving immediately, cool slightly, remove from pans, wrap well, and chill. To re-crisp before serving, warm the tarts on a cookie sheet for a few minutes in a 300° oven. Serve warm or room temperature.

Makes 4 dozen 2-inch tarts.

LIGHT COCKTAIL BUFFET FOR 15 TO 20

SMOKED TROUT SPREAD
CAPONATA WITH FRESH GOAT CHEESE AND FRENCH ROUNDS
FOCCACIA WITH GRILLED ONIONS AND TOMATOES

This menu is great for meetings, cocktails before dinner out, or other events where you don't want to fuss with warming items or replenishing. To bulk up the table, add roasted nuts, fruit, cheese, or special olives. This menu won't work for a longer event, where guests might need to make dinner of the buffet.

SMOKED TROUT SPREAD

Other mild smoked white fish or shrimp also work well in this spread.

½ ounce dry wild mushrooms (preferably morels, or mixed)
2 tablespoons butter
4 medium shallots, chopped
2 tablespoons sherry
1 pound cream cheese or Neufchâtel
½ pound smoked trout, boned and flaked
½ cup chopped black olives or Niçoise olives
½ cup sour cream
juice of 1 lemon
dash cayenne pepper
kosher salt and fresh ground black pepper

In a small bowl, pour hot water over the dried mushrooms. Let sit for 5 minutes. Strain and rinse well. In a small sauté pan, melt the butter and add the shallots and sherry. Stir over medium heat for about 2 minutes. Add the mushrooms and sauté until the shallots are translucent.

In a mixer bowl, beat the cream cheese until soft and smooth. Add the rest of the ingredients, including the mushroom mixture, and mix well. Adjust seasonings. Spoon into a serving bowl and refrigerate until serving.

Makes 1½ pounds. Keeps well for 3 to 4 days.

CAPONATA WITH FRESH GOAT CHEESE AND FRENCH BREAD ROUNDS

Caponata is a lovely relish. But it is also a good side dish, particularly with nutty entrées such as the Chicken Salad with Tarragon and Walnuts (page 44).

2 pounds eggplant, cut into ½-inch cubes, salted, and
    drained for 30 minutes
2 cups chopped yellow onions
⅓ cup olive oil
1 cup (about 2 ribs) chopped celery
6 Roma tomatoes, seeded and chopped
2 tablespoons capers, drained and chopped
¼ cup chopped green olives
¼ cup balsamic vinegar
1 tablespoon sugar
kosher salt and black pepper to taste
French bread, about 2 loaves, cut into thin slices and toasted
12 ounces fresh goat cheese (chevre)

In a large sauté pan, cook the eggplant and onions in the olive oil over low heat until they start to soften. Add the celery and tomatoes and cook until soft. Remove from heat. Stir in the capers and olives.

In a small saucepan, heat the vinegar and sugar together and stir until the sugar is dissolved. Stir into the eggplant mixture. Season to taste, going easy on the salt. Refrigerate.

Makes about 3 pounds. Serve with the French bread rounds and goat cheese on the side. Serves 6 to 8 as a side dish. Keeps up to 5 days.

FOCCACIA WITH GRILLED ONIONS AND TOMATOES

Though the tomato-onion combo is my favorite, you can add or substitute toppings such as herbs, other cheeses, sun-dried tomatoes, chopped olives, crumbled sausage, and wilted spinach.

For the dough:
2 tablespoons dry yeast
1 tablespoon sugar
½ cup warm (under 110°) water
1 cup milk
3 cloves garlic, minced
2 tablespoons rosemary leaves, crushed
¼ cup olive oil, plus extra for greasing pan
3 cups all-purpose flour
1 tablespoon salt

For the toppings:
4 Roma tomatoes, sliced thin
1 large yellow onion, sliced thin and sautéed over medium
    high heat with 2 tablespoons olive oil in a grill pan
    or cast iron skillet until caramelized
1 cup grated Parmesan cheese or mozzarella cheese, hot
    paprika, poppy seeds, kosher salt, and fresh ground
    pepper sprinkled to taste

In a mixer bowl, combine yeast, sugar, and water. Let sit until foamy. Meanwhile, warm the milk with the garlic and rosemary. Let cool to room temperature. Add the olive oil and the milk mixture to the yeast mixture. Using the dough hook at low speed, slowly add the flour and salt. Knead slightly with the dough hook or by hand. The dough will be quite sticky. Cover with plastic wrap and let rise in a warm (80°) place until doubled.

Preheat the oven to 375°. Prepare a large baking sheet with cooking spray and olive oil. With oiled hands, press the dough into a rectangle ⅜-inch thick on the baking sheet. Scatter the toppings evenly. Let rise for about 15 minutes. Bake for 15 to 20 minutes, until the bottom crust of the bread is golden and the bread is done. If using a convection oven, cook for 5 minutes without the fan (to boost rising) and turn on the fan for the rest of the cooking.

Cool slightly. Cut into squares with a straight-edged knife rather than a bread knife. For best results, bake the day you are serving. If you need to make it ahead, refrigerate and reheat before serving for about 10 minutes at 300°.

Makes 3 dozen (2-inch) squares.

HEAVY COCKTAIL BUFFET FOR 40 TO 45

SHRIMP ANCHO TORTA
MARINATED GRILLED FLANK STEAK ON FRENCH BREAD WITH GREEN SAUCE
TAPENADE WITH FRESH TUNA
MINIATURE QUICHES
NEW POTATOES AND HARICOTS VERTS WITH CHIPOTLE DIP

This menu is good for parties that last an entire evening—where guests come and go, some making dinner of the spread, others nibbling, some passing it by.

SHRIMP ANCHO TORTA

This recipe may be halved for smaller crowds. The half recipe molds well in a 6-inch round pan. For vegetarian crowds, eliminate the shrimp—it's almost as tasty without. Serve on a platter with a lip, as the sauce can be messy.

For the sauce:
1 tablespoon olive oil
1 large yellow onion, chopped
4 cloves garlic, minced
2 ancho chiles, seeded, stemmed, and chopped
8 Roma tomatoes or 3 beefsteak tomatoes, chopped
kosher salt and fresh black pepper to taste
1 to 3 teaspoons brown sugar

For the shrimp:
25 medium shrimp (about 1 pound), peeled and cleaned
2 tablespoons olive oil
kosher salt and fresh ground black pepper to taste

For the cheese mixture:
2 pounds cream cheese or Neufchâtel cheese
1 pound fresh goat cheese (chevre)
kosher salt and fresh ground black pepper to taste

For the garnish:
cilantro leaves
½ cup pepitas (green pumpkin seeds), toasted at 350° for about 5 minutes or until they start to puff up and hop around

In a small saucepan, sauté the onion and garlic in the olive oil until soft. Add the chiles and tomatoes. Cover with water and simmer until the sauce is thick and brick red, adding water if it reduces too quickly. Season to taste with salt and pepper. Add brown sugar to balance the bitter chiles. Set aside.

In a small sauté pan, cook the shrimp in olive oil over medium heat until opaque. Chop the shrimp, saving one for garnish if you like. Refrigerate.

Beat together the cream cheese and goat cheese in a large mixing bowl until smooth and soft. Season with salt and pepper.

To assemble, line a 10-inch round pan with plastic wrap. Spread half of the cheese mixture on the bottom. Top with half of the sauce and all but ¼ cup of the chopped shrimp, then add the rest of the cheese mixture. Smooth the top, cover with plastic, and refrigerate for at least an hour before serving.

To serve, unwrap torta and center an inverted platter on top. Carefully flip the pan and platter over so that the torta is sitting upright. Lift off the pan, remove the plastic and smooth the top and sides of the torta with a spatula. Immediately before serving, garnish with the sauce, cilantro, remaining shrimp, and pepitas. Serve with 3 or 4 boxes of crackers.

Makes enough for 30 to 45.

MARINATED GRILLED FLANK STEAK WITH GREEN SAUCE

1 cup dry red wine
3 cloves garlic, minced
2 tablespoons Dijon mustard
3 tablespoons soy sauce
5 pounds flank steak, trimmed of fat and membrane and
    pierced with a knife point every 2 inches

For the green sauce:
1 cup Italian (flat) parsley leaves
12 ounces fresh spinach, rinsed well and trimmed of stems
½ cup fresh basil or cilantro leaves
½ cup olive oil
¼ cup capers
1 tablespoon balsamic vinegar or sherry vinegar
1 teaspoon lemon juice
kosher salt and fresh ground black pepper to taste

4 loaves of French bread or ciabatta, sliced at an angle,
    brushed with olive oil and toasted or grilled

Combine the red wine, garlic, mustard, and soy in a pan or heavy plastic bag. Add steak and marinate, refrigerated, for 3 to 12 hours.

To grill the flank steak medium rare, cook each side over a hot grill for 4 to 5 minutes. Check doneness by making a small incision in the middle of the meat, returning it to the grill or finishing it in the oven if necessary. Let the meat sit for about 10 minutes before cutting thin slices at an angle across the grain.

Combine the green sauce ingredients in the bowl of a processor and purée until smooth. Season to taste.

A few minutes before serving, spread the green sauce on the bread and top with flank steak slices. The meat juices will soak into the bread and they will not look pretty if they sit too long. Another choice would be to serve the sauce in a bowl and the meat on a platter with the bread on the side.

Makes 50 to 60 open-face sandwiches.

TAPENADE WITH FRESH TUNA
AND PITA CHIPS

½ pound fresh tuna steak—yellow fin, albacore, or ahi
1 tablespoon olive oil
1 tablespoon lime juice
4 (15-ounce) cans chickpeas, drained and rinsed
1 red bell pepper, chopped
2 cloves garlic, minced
lemon juice to taste
¼ cup olive oil, more if needed
½ cup pitted calamata olives
kosher salt and fresh ground black pepper to taste
about 10 pieces of pita bread

To cook the tuna, brush the steak with olive oil and lime juice. Grill or broil until it barely flakes, about 6 to 8 minutes. Break up with a fork. Set aside.

In the processor with a steel blade, combine the rest of the ingredients. Purée until smooth. Add the flaked tuna and pulse until just incorporated, but not annihilated. Add more olive oil, lemon, salt, and pepper if needed.

Slice the pita rounds into 8 wedges (if small, use more bread, cut into 6). Toast until crisp. Serve on the side.

Makes about 2½ pounds.

MINIATURE QUICHES

Since quiche was one of the everyday items at Lilly & Co., I grew to think of it as comfort food. Once in a blue moon, I would have a slice or snack on a miniature quiche and be reminded of how very tasty and elegant it is.

1½ or 2 batches Short Crust Pastry, page 30

For the filling:
5 large eggs
1¼ cups heavy cream
⅔ cup milk
1 teaspoon kosher salt
fresh ground black pepper
1½ - 2 cups grated cheese (Swiss, Gruyere, Monterey Jack, or sharp Cheddar)
any fillings such as: Roma tomatoes in thin quarter-slices, fresh spinach (cooked, squeezed dry, and chopped), mushrooms (chopped, sautéed, and drained), leeks (chopped, washed well, and sautéed), chopped cooked bacon

To prepare the pastry, roll the disk to ⅛-inch thickness. Cut into 2½-inch circles and place in small shallow tart pans sprayed with nonstick spray (I use British jelly pans, which might be hard to find. Any small, shallow pan will work well). Prick the bottoms of the shells gently with a fork. Refrigerate.

Preheat the oven to 375°. In a medium bowl, whisk together the eggs, cream, milk, salt, and pepper. To assemble, put about 1 teaspoon of the prepared fillings in the bottom of each shell, then top with a generous pinch (about 1 tablespoon) of cheese. Carefully pour or spoon the egg mixture into each tart, filling and coming as close to the top of the shell as possible. Bake for 14 to 16 minutes, until the filling is puffed up and golden brown. Run a paring knife around the sides of each tart before removing it from the pan. If the crust looks soggy at all, bake another 2 to 3 minutes on a baking sheet to crisp. Refrigerate if not serving immediately. The quiches are good hot or at room temperature. Either way, they have a better texture if they are re-crisped after they have been chilled.

Makes about 6 dozen.

SHORT CRUST PASTRY

Many people find that they have a more forgiving dough and a flakier crust if they substitute shortening for some of the butter. I like to use butter for the flavor. Either way, the secret to good pastry is in how it's handled.

3½ cups all-purpose flour
2 sticks (½ pound) unsalted butter, cut into ½-inch cubes and kept cold
1 teaspoon salt
about ¾ cup cold water

Combine the flour and the salt in the processor bowl with the steel blade. Scatter the butter evenly around on the flour mixture. Pulse quickly just until the mixture resembles coarse breadcrumbs, being careful not to melt the butter. Pour ½ cup of the water (no ice) around the bowl on top of the mixture and pulse again until it is barely incorporated and the dough begins to pull away from the sides of the processor bowl. If needed, add more water, very little at a time, until the dough just holds together when pressed between two fingers. Turn out onto a lightly floured board and knead gently and quickly into a ball. Cut into 2 parts, flatten into disks, wrap in plastic and chill for at least 30 minutes.

To roll the dough, spread flour sparingly on your work surface. Also brush the rolling pin with a little flour. Roll once, turn 90°, sprinkle the surface and the top of the pastry with a little more flour, and repeat, working quickly, until you form a circle of dough about ⅛-inch thick. Form or cut as desired for recipe. Refrigerate again before using.

Note that any of the following things can make your pastry tough: too much water, butter that's not cold, excess flour in rolling, and over-handling. To use leftover pastry scraps, brush off extra flour and fold neatly in layers to make a disk, chilling again before rolling.

Makes 2 single tart crusts or 4 dozen miniature tart shells.

NEW POTATOES AND HARICOTS VERTS WITH CHIPOTLE DIP

For the dip:
1 pound cream cheese or Neufchâtel cheese
¾ cup buttermilk or sour cream
½ cup tomato paste
1 teaspoon dried oregano
½ teaspoon dried dill
1 teaspoon ground cumin
3 cloves garlic, minced
3 chipotle peppers, packed in adobo sauce, chopped fine
    or puréed
kosher salt and black pepper to taste
brown sugar as needed

40 to 50 size "B" (medium) new potatoes
3 pounds haricots verts (French green beans) or harvester
    green beans

To make the dip, combine all of the ingredients in a blender and purée until smooth. If the dip tastes a little bitter, add 1 teaspoon brown sugar to bring it into balance.

Cook the new potatoes in a large saucepan of water, covered, until a knife goes into them without resistance (but not too easily), 20 to 25 minutes. Cut into quarters lengthwise. Cook the haricots in boiling water for about 4 minutes (taste for doneness), drain and plunge into ice water to keep the color and crispness. Cook harvesters the same way for 6 to 7 minutes.

If you prefer to roast the new potatoes instead of boiling, slice them into quarters lengthwise and toss in olive oil. Spread the slices on a baking sheet prepared with cooking spray. Salt and pepper the potatoes and bake them at 375° until nicely browned, 20 to 30 minutes.

Arrange the vegetables on a platter with the dip in a bowl.

fORK fOOD

VEGETARIAN FEAST FOR 8

VEGETABLE GOAT CHEESE TORTA IN PHYLLO PASTRY
FRENCH LENTILS WITH BUTTERNUT SQUASH
CHERRY TOMATOES WITH FETA AND MINT
WHITE CHOCOLATE OAT BARS

The vegetarian feast is easy on your oven space. There is a lot that can be done in advance. The only thing that I would serve hot, though it's not required, is the Vegetable Goat Cheese Torta.

Serve the meal with good bread, a plain French or Italian loaf. You could add a very simple salad of mixed greens with vinaigrette and toasted nuts.

It's easy to prepare the ingredients for the torta a day or even two ahead, except for the spinach, which will taste better if freshly prepared. Still, the assembly takes time and space and should be done well before guests arrive.

VEGETABLE GOAT CHEESE TORTA IN PHYLLO PASTRY

The combination of vegetables in layers makes this very colorful and healthful. The potatoes and fresh goat cheese are heavenly together. The assembly is easy if all of the layers are prepared in advance. Peel the potatoes only if you have nothing better to do.

2 large yellow onions, sliced
3 tablespoons olive oil
2 red bell peppers, sliced
½ pound mushrooms, sliced
2 large russet potatoes
12 ounces fresh spinach, trimmed of stems and washed well
1 pound mild fresh goat cheese, whipped soft
2 tablespoons basil purée (see page 9)
5 to 6 Roma tomatoes or 3 beefsteak tomatoes, sliced
3 cups grated Monterey Jack cheese
kosher salt and fresh ground black pepper
freshly grated nutmeg
1 stick butter, melted, more if needed
phyllo pastry, about 12 sheets
about ¾ cup grated Parmesan cheese

In a large sauté pan over medium heat, cook the onions in olive oil for about 2 minutes. Add the peppers and mushrooms and cook until soft. Set aside in a colander to drain for at least 15 minutes. Slice the potatoes ¼-inch thick and boil until just done, about 5 minutes. Drain and set aside. In a sauté pan over medium heat, stir the spinach with very little water until wilted. Dry well and set aside.

Butter (or use non-stick spray) a 9 X 13 X 2-inch baking pan. Lay down sheets of phyllo, buttering each layer and staggering the sheets to cover the bottom and come up the sides to the edge of the pan, until 4 layers of thick. Cover the remaining sheets with a towel to prevent drying.

Preheat oven to 350°. Combine the goat cheese and the basil and spread the mixture on the phyllo, completely covering the bottom. Next, neatly lay the potatoes on top of the goat cheese. Salt and pepper liberally. Sprinkle with fresh nutmeg. On top of the potatoes, lay out the onions, peppers, and mushrooms. Spread the spinach next, then more salt, pepper, and nutmeg. Top with tomato slices and Jack cheese. Cover with 5 sheets of phyllo, each buttered. Sprinkle with Parmesan. Bake until the pastry is golden brown, and the vegetables heated through, about 35 minutes.

Serves 12 as a side dish, 8 to 9 as a main course.

FRENCH LENTILS WITH BUTTERNUT SQUASH

These lentils are great at room temperature but are also delicious warm. All of the items except the spinach can be prepared a day ahead. Since spinach begins to taste metallic after 2 days, wash, wilt, and combine it with the other ingredients the day you serve it. If butternut squash is out of season, substitute about 8 medium new potatoes, boiled until just done (about 25 minutes) and sliced ½ inch thick.

1 pound dry lentils, preferably French green
1 yellow onion (peeled and whole) studded with 10 whole cloves
12 ounces fresh spinach, picked, rinsed, wilted in very little water over low heat, drained well and chopped
¼ medium red onion, very thinly sliced
4 pounds butternut squash, halved and seeded, baked at 350°, face down on a greased baking sheet until easily pierced with a knife, about 40 minutes
3 cloves garlic, minced
zest of 2 well-washed lemons, removed with a peeler then cut into needle strips
juice of 2 lemons
½ cup olive oil
1 tablespoon balsamic vinegar
kosher salt and fresh ground black pepper to taste

In a medium pot, simmer the lentils in water with the studded onion for 30 to 40 minutes, until barely tender. Drain the lentils and discard the onion. *Note:* if you use regular brown lentils, they will have a somewhat chalky texture and should be rinsed briefly after cooking.

Peel the cooked butternut squash and cut into ½-inch pieces. Whisk together the garlic, lemon zest and juice, oil, vinegar, and salt and pepper to make the dressing. Combine with the lentils, spinach, red onion, and squash. Serve warm or at room temperature.

Serves 10 to 12.

CHERRY TOMATOES WITH FETA AND MINT

Easy and delicious.

3 pints cherry tomatoes, sliced in half through the stem
3 medium shallots, thinly sliced
⅔ cup feta cheese, crumbled
2 to 3 tablespoons fresh mint leaves, chopped
3 tablespoons olive oil
fresh ground black pepper and kosher salt to taste

Toss all of the ingredients together right before serving. The ingredients themselves may be prepared (except for the mint) the day before and refrigerated separately.

This dish is also terrific made with cocktail tomatoes or teardrop yellow tomatoes. I prefer spearmint, but other mint varieties work just as well.

Serves 8 to 10.

WHITE CHOCOLATE OAT BARS

One recipe makes more than enough for 8 guests, but extras are great to have around. They keep well, especially if they are refrigerated.

For the pastry:
2 sticks (½ pound) unsalted butter
½ cup sugar
½ cup brown sugar
½ teaspoon kosher salt
1 teaspoon vanilla extract
1 egg yolk
1 cup unbleached all-purpose flour
1 cup quick-cooking oats (see note below)
1 cup toasted sliced almonds, roughly chopped

For the topping:
½ pound white chocolate, good quality, such as Callebaut
shaved bittersweet chocolate, about ¼ cup (use a peeler)

Preheat oven to 350°. In a mixer, cream the butter. Add the sugars. When well mixed, add the salt, vanilla, egg yolk, flour, oats, and almonds. Spread the mixture in a 9 X 13-inch cake pan prepared with non-stick cooking spray. Bake for 12 to 15 minutes, until medium brown. Cool slightly.

Meanwhile, melt the white chocolate gently in a double boiler. Spread evenly over the top of the pastry. While still hot, sprinkle with the chocolate shavings and with the tip of a knife, quickly swirl the dark chocolate in with the white to make marble patterns. Refrigerate until chocolate is set before cutting.

Note: if you use oats other than quick-cooking, the crust will taste like baked paper.

Makes 2 dozen (2-inch) square bars.

DINNER FOR 10

ORANGE ACHIOTE SHRIMP ON SAFFRON RICE WITH AVOCADO VERDE SAUCE
SALAD WITH CHIPOTLE DRESSING
ALMOND FLAN

This dinner doesn't have to be piping hot to be delicious. If you want more
on the table, add an appetizer of the Ancho Torta (page 26) or start with a nice cold
Gazpacho (page 108).

ORANGE-ACHIOTE SHRIMP ON SAFFRON RICE

Achiote has a subtle flavor that is hard to describe. It lends a lovely color to this dish. Achiote powder is sometimes difficult to find. I have had the best luck at Mexican markets, where it is packaged as little bricks.

You can make the Avocado Verde Sauce, page 59, while the shrimp marinates.

For the marinade:
2 tablespoons brown sugar
juice and zest of 2 oranges (no white pith)
¾ teaspoon achiote powder
¾ cup canola or safflower oil
3 cloves garlic, minced
kosher salt and fresh ground black pepper to taste
3 to 3½ pounds medium (21 to 25 count) fresh shrimp,
    peeled and cleaned

For the rice:
3 cups aromatic rice (Texmati or Basmati)
1 cup white wine
5 cups water
¼ teaspoon saffron threads
2 teaspoons kosher salt
2 tablespoons butter
1 large yellow onion, chopped
1 ear fresh corn, stripped from cob
1 cup golden raisins
1 cup toasted pecan pieces
fresh ground black pepper to taste
lime wedges for garnish

Combine all marinade ingredients in a blender and purée until smooth. Toss with shrimp and marinate in the refrigerator for at least 1 and up to 8 hours.

To make the rice, combine the wine, water, saffron, and salt in a large saucepan. Bring to a boil, reduce to a simmer and cover to cook for about 10 minutes, until just soft, but not mushy. Meanwhile, in a sauté pan, melt the butter and add the onions and corn. Cook over medium heat until soft, 5 to 7 minutes. Stir in raisins and pecans and add to the rice. If necessary, add salt and pepper.

While the rice cooks, preheat oven to 350°. Arrange shrimp in lines on a baking sheet so they touch (they keep their shape better this way). Lightly salt and pepper. Bake until slightly firm and opaque, especially where they touch, about 8 minutes. Check frequently so as not to overcook. Serve shrimp on top of rice, hot or room temperature. Drizzle with Avocado Verde Sauce.

Serves 8 to 10.

SALAD WITH CHIPOTLE DRESSING

about 1 pound mesclun salad mix (baby mixed greens)
1 bunch asparagus (about 30 spears)
¼ cup red onion, sliced thin
2 red bell peppers, roasted, seeded, peeled, and sliced
    (see note page 9)
2 ripe avocados, sliced
1 cup Mexican cojita cheese (feta may be substituted),
    crumbled

For the dressing:
½ cup mayonnaise, fresh or good quality (reduced fat is fine)
½ cup buttermilk
¼ cup tomato paste
½ teaspoon dried oregano
¼ teaspoon dried dill
2 cloves garlic, minced
2 chipotle peppers (canned in adobo sauce), fewer if you
    desire less spice
kosher salt (about 1 teaspoon) and pepper to taste
lemon juice or sugar, to taste

Pick and rinse the greens and gently dry. Blanch asparagus spears in boiling water for about 2 minutes, immediately plunging into a bowl of ice water to preserve flavor and crunch. Drain well. Cut into bite size pieces and combine with other salad ingredients. Dress lightly right before serving.

Combine the dressing ingredients in a blender and purée until smooth. If a bit sweet, add a touch of lemon juice. If bitter, a pinch of sugar to balance. The dressing recipe makes more than you will probably need for this amount of salad. It will keep well, however, covered in the refrigerator, for about a week. Also remember that if you serve the dressing on the side, you will need to have more on hand than if you toss the salad before serving.

Serves about 10.

ALMOND FLAN

For the caramel:
2 cups sugar
1 cup water

For the custard:
2 cups milk
3 cups heavy cream
1¼ cups sugar
4 ounces cream cheese, soft
4 large eggs
5 additional egg yolks
1 teaspoon vanilla
½ teaspoon almond extract
¾ cup sliced almonds, toasted until golden brown,
    cooled, and finely ground

Put 12 (4-ounce) custard cups in a roasting or baking pan and fill the pan with hot water until it reaches halfway up the sides of the cups.

In a heavy saucepan, combine the sugar and water for caramel. Bring to a boil and cook over high heat until the mixture starts to brown. Remove from heat and pour into each custard cup until about ¼-inch deep. Set cups aside until the caramel is hard—something that should be checked with a spoon, not a fingertip.

Preheat oven to 325°. To make the custard, heat the milk, sugar, and cream together in a saucepan until bubbles form around the edge and the mixture is hot to the touch. Remove from heat and set aside to cool slightly. In a large mixing bowl, beat the cream cheese until fluffy. Add the eggs and yolks one at a time, scraping the sides of the bowl after each addition. Add the almonds and extracts. Scrape down the sides of the bowl and make sure the mixture is smooth. While mixing on slow speed, pour in the milk mixture slowly. Divide the custard among the prepared cups. Cover the pan with foil and bake until set, about 25 minutes (see note page 9).

Refrigerate flans until serving. To unmold, run a knife around the edge of the flan and invert onto a plate with a lip, letting the caramel syrup drip from the cup to the plate. Refrigerate until serving. The flans can be made up to 3 days ahead, and they will keep about a week.

Makes 12 flans.

LUNCH FOR 12

CHICKEN SALAD WITH DRIED CHERRIES AND MINT
or CHICKEN SALAD WITH TARRAGON AND WALNUTS
LILLY PASTA SALAD
CORN AND AVOCADO SALAD
SPINACH AND WILD RICE SALAD WITH ORANGE HOISIN
LEMON TARTS

This menu is a favorite for a "ladies' lunch." If you want to simplify
preparations, you could eliminate the chicken salad. Instead,
grill or roast some chicken breasts to toss with the Orange Hoisin
and serve with the spinach salad.

CHICKEN SALAD WITH DRIED CHERRIES AND MINT

The mayo-yogurt combination makes this chicken salad a little bit lower in fat. The mint makes it fresh and perky, but other fresh herbs will work well when mint is unavailable. Unlike the tarragon chicken salad, this one holds up well overnight.

10 whole (7-ounce) skinless chicken breasts
⅓ cup fresh mayonnaise (page 45) or store-bought
⅓ cup plain yogurt
⅔ cup chopped celery
¼ cup finely chopped red onion
1½ tablespoons fresh mint leaves, chopped
1¼ cup sliced almonds, toasted about 6 minutes until light brown
¼ cup dried cherries, plumped in hot water for 1 minute, drained, and chopped
kosher salt and fresh ground black pepper to taste

Preheat oven to 350°. Lightly coat a baking sheet with cooking spray and lay the chicken breasts flat. Season with salt and pepper and bake for 10 to 12 minutes, until the breast feels firm and springs back when touched. Cool slightly. Trim fat and membranes and cut chicken into ½-inch cubes.

Combine the rest of the ingredients in a medium bowl. Add the chicken breast pieces and toss until well coated. Serve cold. Makes about 4 pounds.

CHICKEN SALAD WITH TARRAGON AND WALNUTS

The fresh mayonnaise is what makes this chicken salad special.

4 to 5 bone-in chicken breasts (about 6 pounds)
3 to 4 tablespoons dry tarragon leaves
½ cup walnut pieces
kosher salt and fresh ground black pepper to taste
½ to ¾ cup fresh mayonnaise (page 45) or store-bought
2 tablespoons warm water

In a large saucepan or stockpot, cover the chicken breasts with room temperature water. Bring to a boil then reduce to a slow simmer. After 10 minutes, remove the pan from the heat and let the chicken sit in the cooking liquid for another 10 minutes to gently finish cooking. Remove the chicken from the water and let cool enough to handle. Remove bones, tendons, and skins. If desired, save the liquid and the bones and skins for stock. Cut the chicken into large chunks and set aside.

In the bottom of a medium bowl, whisk ½ cup of the mayonnaise with the tarragon, walnuts, salt, and pepper. Add a little water if needed, for extra creaminess. Toss chicken pieces gently with the mayonnaise mixture. Do not over-mix or the chicken will fall to shreds. Correct seasonings, add more mayonnaise if needed, and serve the same day it is mixed. Leftover salad is best used for sandwiches; the texture suffers overnight.

Serves 8 to 10.

FRESH MAYONNAISE

4 egg yolks (see note on Spicy Remoulade recipe, page 65)
3 tablespoons whole grain mustard
⅔ cup canola or safflower oil
⅓ cup extra virgin olive oil
2 tablespoons red wine vinegar
kosher salt and fresh ground pepper to taste

Place the egg yolks and mustard in the bowl of the food processor. Process with the metal blade until the mixture is pale yellow. Combine the safflower and olive oil and, with the machine running, add half of the mixed oils very slowly in a thin stream. Add the vinegar, then add the rest of the oil in the same manner. Season to taste. If the mayonnaise is stiff, add 2 to 3 tablespoons of warm water to make it creamy. Leftover mayonnaise will keep for about 10 days, refrigerated in a tightly covered container.

Note: if your mayonnaise curdles, don't throw it away. Remove it from the processor bowl and set aside. Combine 1 egg yolk with a teaspoon of mustard in the processor bowl. Process until pale then add the broken mayonnaise slowly (as the oil was added to the yolks before) until emulsified.

Makes about 1½ cups.

LILLY PASTA SALAD

Children loved this pasta, despite the fresh basil and balsamic vinegar, ate tons of it over the 14 years of business. More than one former customer has called for the recipe since I closed the Lilly, desperate to make the pasta for a sick child who was hungry for nothing else.

If you don't have good fresh pasta, use dried and cut back on the dressing. This particular pasta salad, once dressed, is not a great leftover the next day.

2 pounds fresh fusilli noodles
1 ripe avocado, cut into ½-inch pieces
3 to 4 Roma tomatoes, chopped

For the dressing:
⅔ cup canola or safflower oil
⅓ cup balsamic vinegar
2 teaspoons basil purée (see note page 9)
1½ teaspoons kosher salt
fresh ground black pepper to taste

Cook the pasta in a large pot of boiling water according to package instructions until tender to taste. Drain and rinse with cold water until cool.

Combine the dressing ingredients and whisk until emulsified. Toss pasta with about ¾ of the dressing. Adjust seasoning and add tomatoes, avocado, and more dressing if needed.

Leftover dressing will keep about 2 weeks refrigerated.

Makes 10 to 12 side servings.

CORN AND AVOCADO SALAD

No matter how much of this dish we made, we always
seemed to sell out before lunch was over. Often, the staff
got to it before the customers did. The lime and avocado
play on the sweetness of the corn.

12 ears fresh corn, husks and silks removed
3 avocados, cut into ½-inch pieces
¼ cup lime juice
1 tablespoon raspberry vinegar
¾ cup canola or safflower oil
2 tablespoons cilantro leaves, chopped
kosher salt and fresh ground black pepper to taste

In a large pot, cook the ears of corn in boiling water for about
10 minutes. Cool. Remove corn kernels from the cobs with a
small knife. Toss the corn with the other ingredients.

Makes 10 to 12 servings. Keeps 2 days if refrigerated and covered well.

SPINACH AND WILD RICE SALAD WITH ORANGE HOISIN

For the salad:
2 cups uncooked wild rice
12 ounces fresh spinach, picked, washed, and sliced
    into ribbons
1 small head radicchio, core removed and sliced thin
3 Roma tomatoes, cut into small pieces
¼ pound mushrooms, sliced
¼ cup red onion, sliced thin
1 red bell pepper, sliced

For the dressing:
zest and juice of 1 orange
¾ cup canola or safflower oil
½ cup soy sauce
2 tablespoons brown sugar
½ cup hoisin sauce (available in Chinese markets)
½ cup rice wine vinegar
fresh ground black pepper to taste

In a large saucepan, combine the wild rice with 8 cups water. Bring to a boil and reduce to simmer. Cook uncovered, adding water if necessary, until done, about 25 minutes. The rice grains will have burst slightly and should be firm, but not crunchy. Drain and let cool to room temperature. Combine with the other salad ingredients in a large bowl.

To make the dressing, combine the ingredients in a blender and purée until smooth. Adjust seasonings to taste. Toss salad with about 1 cup of the dressing right before serving, adding more to taste if you like. Leftover dressing will keep for about 2 weeks in the refrigerator.

If you prefer more crunch in your salads, add toasted sliced almonds, fried wonton strips, or chow mein noodles to taste.

Makes 10 side servings or 6 main course salads.

LEMON TARTS

A British friend of mine left his widow a poem when he died that described his love for her as greater than his love for lemon tarts. Simple and luscious, they are the best British arrival except for maybe the Beatles.

For the lemon curd:
1 cup sugar
1 stick (¼ pound) butter
grated zest and juice of 3 lemons
3 eggs, beaten

For the pastry:
1 batch Short Crust Pastry, page 30

For the topping:
1 pint heavy cream
1 teaspoon vanilla extract

To make the curd, combine the sugar, butter, zest, juice, and eggs in a non-reactive double boiler. Cook over medium heat, stirring often to prevent the eggs from curdling, until the mixture thickens, 30 to 45 minutes. It will also thicken more as it cools. Remove from heat and cover with plastic wrap directly touching the surface of the curd. Refrigerate until cold.

To make the tart shells, roll the pastry on a lightly floured board to about ⅛-inch thick. Carefully lift the pastry to release any parts that might be stuck to the pastry board. Cut into 36 2-inch circles, working quickly so as not to warm the dough, and place the circles in shallow, wide tart pans (British "jelly" pans work well). Prick twice with a fork and weigh down with individual metal tart pans or weights on foil. Chill for a few minutes while you preheat the oven to 375°. Bake until golden, about 12 minutes. Cool and fill each tart with 1 to 2 tablespoons lemon curd.

Whip the cream with the vanilla to soft peaks, until it barely holds a shape. Using a pastry bag, pipe the whipped cream onto the lemon curd. To make a rosette, keep the tip close to the surface to make a circle, lifting the tip off sideways as you reach the center. There will be more than enough whipped cream, which is never a problem in our house.

Note: I like to put together these tarts as needed. They can be little troublemakers once assembled—they will hog your refrigerator space and pick up other food odors.

Makes 3 dozen.

SOUTHWESTERN DINNER FOR 12

ENCHILADAS VERDES WITH CHICKEN AND CHEESE
CORN TIMBALE
ROSARIO'S BLACK BEANS
BLACK PEPPER BROWNIES

Most of this dinner can be done ahead of time. It's easy to heat and serve and requires very little last-minute attention. You will need oven space for the enchiladas and timbale.

If you want to add an item to the table, try a leaf lettuce salad with Chipotle Dressing (page 41).

For appetizers, try the Ancho Torta (page 26), the Avocado and Peach Pico de Gallo (page 17) or the Pepper Cheese Spread (page 13).

ENCHILADAS VERDES WITH CHICKEN AND CHEESE

12 large bone-in chicken breast halves (about 8 pounds raw)
30 corn tortillas
oil for frying (corn, canola, safflower, or other vegetable oil)
½ recipe verde sauce
6 to 7 cups grated Monterey Jack cheese

Place the chicken breasts in a large stockpot and cover with water. Bring to a boil and reduce to a simmer. Turn off the heat after 10 minutes, but let the chicken sit in the cooking water for another 10 minutes, then remove from hot water and set aside. When cool enough to handle, peel the skin from the breasts and discard. Peel the meat away from the bone and pull apart into large pieces. Set aside.

Meanwhile, in ¼ inch of oil in a medium skillet over medium heat, quickly fry the tortillas on both sides, one at a time, just until soft. Do not crisp them or they will break when rolled. Drain well on paper towels.

Preheat oven to 350°. Coat the bottoms of 2 roasting pans (I prefer glass or ceramic) with a thin layer of verde sauce. Spread out the fried tortillas on a clean work surface. In assembly-line fashion, put about ¼ cup verde sauce, ½ cup cooked chicken, and a sprinkling of cheese down the center of each tortilla. Roll the filled tortillas into compact tubes and place them seam side down in the pans (if you are serving later, stop at this step, wrap, and refrigerate). To finish cooking, cover them completely with verde sauce and sprinkle with cheese. Bake for 25 to 35 minutes, until heated through.

Makes 30 enchiladas, enough for 12 to 15 guests.

VERDE SAUCE

10 pounds fresh tomatillos, shucked of papery skins and
     washed very well in warm water
2 large yellow onions, peeled and cut in half
10 to 12 garlic cloves, peeled
2 poblano peppers, seeded and stemmed
about ¼ cup cilantro leaves
juice of about 3 limes
kosher salt and fresh black pepper to taste
1 teaspoon sugar, if necessary

Combine whole tomatillos, onions, garlic, and poblanos in a tall stockpot. Cover with cold water and cook on high heat until the tomatillos turn dull green, which usually happens before the water boils. Remove from heat and drain immediately, careful not to burst the tomatillos. Cool slightly, then purée along with the remaining ingredients until smooth. Add the sugar if the sauce tastes too tart.

Makes enough for about 60 enchiladas. This sauce freezes well, but needs to be puréed again after thawing. It is great to have around for dips.

CORN TIMBALE

This recipe is the result of a happy accident at the Lilly. Kendel adapted a timbale recipe to give it a southwestern bent and we swooned over the final product. When I asked her to write down what she had done, she opened the reference and realized that she had gotten virtually everything backwards; what she did in no way resembled what she had intended. It became our most popular dish.

Forget that the ingredients are rich. Make it with no low-fat substitutes and you will have no regrets. And use fresh corn. An 11 X 16-inch roasting pan is the best size. If you use a smaller pan, you might need to cover it with foil halfway through to prevent browning.

For the custard:
8 large eggs, lightly beaten
6 ears of fresh corn, stripped of silks, rinsed, and kernels
    cut from cobs
1 teaspoon kosher salt
½ teaspoon pepper
dash Tabasco sauce
3 tablespoons sugar
about ¼ cup cilantro leaves, chopped (no stems)
1½ cups grated Monterey Jack cheese
⅔ cup fresh breadcrumbs (day-old French bread is perfect)
1 quart heavy cream
1 poblano pepper, roasted (see note page 9), peeled, seeded
    and chopped

For the topping:
½ cup fresh goat cheese, crumbled
fresh ground black pepper

Preheat the oven to 350°. In a medium bowl, mix the custard ingredients well. Pour into pan, top with goat cheese and pepper, and bake uncovered for 40 to 50 minutes, until set. It will puff up, indicating that the eggs are cooked. Cover the pan if the timbale gets too brown before the custard is cooked.

Makes 12 to 14 side servings.

ROSARIO'S BLACK BEANS

We used to make a soup of these beans by adding more chicken stock and puréeing the whole thing. Serve the soup with the same garnish.

4 cups raw black turtle beans, sorted to check for rocks, rinsed
1 quart chicken stock
1 teaspoon baking soda
1 medium yellow onion, chopped
5 Roma tomatoes, chopped
3 cloves garlic, minced
½ teaspoon cumin seeds, toasted in a dry skillet until fragrant and crushed, or 1 teaspoon ground cumin
2 tablespoons cilantro leaves, chopped
kosher salt and fresh black pepper to taste
lemon wheels and sour cream for garnish

In a large saucepan, cover the beans with chicken stock. Add the baking soda and bring to a boil. Reduce to a simmer and add the onion, tomatoes, garlic, and cumin. Add water as needed, but only as much as it takes to continue cooking. When the beans are tender, usually after about 2 to 3 hours, season to taste with cilantro, salt, and pepper.

Makes about 3 quarts.

BLACK PEPPER BROWNIES

This recipe was adapted from a Maida Heatter recipe. The black pepper gives the brownies a zip and a lift and is a perfect match for really good quality chocolate. Our favorite for this recipe is Callebaut.

3 sticks (¾ pound) butter (add ½ teaspoon salt if using unsalted butter)
2 cups light brown sugar
2 teaspoons instant coffee crystals
2 teaspoons vanilla extract
2 teaspoons finely ground black pepper
6 large eggs
½ pound (8 ounces) good quality bittersweet chocolate, melted
1½ cups all-purpose flour
1 cup pecan pieces

Preheat oven to 350°. Butter a 9 X 13-inch cake pan. Line the bottom with waxed paper and butter the paper.

In a large mixer bowl, beat the butter until soft. Add the brown sugar and cream until fluffy. In a small bowl, dissolve the coffee crystals in the vanilla and add to the butter and sugar. Add the black pepper, the eggs (one at a time), then the melted chocolate, the flour, and finally the pecans. Do not over mix. Pour into the prepared baking pan and level the top of the mixture with a rubber spatula. Check after 30 minutes. The brownies will also puff slightly in the middle. Moist crumbs should cling to a tester toothpick; it should not be clean and dry. Re-check the brownies every 2 to 3 minutes as they come close to being done, as they are much tastier if not over baked. We also found that the brownies had the best texture if put in the freezer for a few minutes straight from the oven. Cool slightly and run a knife around the edge of the pan before cutting.

Makes 24 brownies.

SALMON DINNER FOR 15

ANCHO-GLAZED SALMON WITH MANGO BUERRE BLANC
   OR AVOCADO VERDE SAUCE
ORZO WITH FRESH BASIL
ROASTED VEGETABLES
CRÈME BRÛLÉE

This dinner is great served at room temperature, meaning that you can do the dirty work before guests arrive. If you want to fill in the table, make a simple salad of mixed greens with nuts and vinaigrette.

ANCHO-GLAZED SALMON WITH MANGO BUERRE BLANC
OR AVOCADO VERDE SAUCE

This dish is delicious hot, but just is good at room temperature. Leftovers make a great salad. The glaze may be made 3 days ahead and rubbed on the salmon up to 3 hours before cooking.

5 to 6 pounds fresh salmon fillets (whole sides or cut portions), with skin, bones removed

For the glaze:
1 cup dry white wine
2 tablespoons butter
1 ancho chile, seeds and stem removed, cut into strips
1 medium mango, peeled and sliced, slightly unripe is fine
2 (2-inch) strips of lemon zest (yellow part only)
juice of 1 lemon
2 teaspoons brown sugar
kosher salt and fresh ground black pepper to taste

For the sauce:
1 cup dry white wine
⅓ cup raspberry vinegar
2 (2-inch strips) lemon zest (yellow part only)
1 mango, peeled and sliced
2 sticks (½ pound) butter, cut into small pieces
pinch cayenne pepper
kosher salt and fresh ground black pepper to taste
lemon juice and brown sugar to taste if needed

To make the glaze, combine the white wine, butter, ancho, mango, and lemon zest in a small heavy saucepan. Bring to a boil, reduce to a simmer, and cook until the mixture starts to turn a brick red color, 30 to 40 minutes. Add the lemon juice and brown sugar. Purée in a blender until smooth. Season to taste.

To make the sauce, combine the wine, vinegar, and zest in a small heavy saucepan. Boil until reduced by half. Remove the zest and add the mango. Remove from heat and let sit until the mango is soft. Add the butter little by little, whisking to fully incorporate each piece until emulsified. Purée the mixture in the blender. Add and adjust seasonings and serve at room temperature. Do not reheat the sauce—it will separate. If needed, add a little lemon juice or 1 teaspoon brown sugar to taste.

To cook the salmon preheat oven to 375°. Place the salmon skin side down on a shallow baking dish covered with foil. Gently score the top (by cutting about ½-inch deep) of the salmon, or cut into individual servings if desired. Rub the glaze into the cuts and completely cover the surface of the fish. Roast until the flesh is slightly firm and flakes somewhat easily, about 10 to 15 minutes depending on thickness and the size of the fillet. It will cook faster if you cut it into servings before cooking.

To serve, gently run a flat spatula between the fish and the skin. Carefully slide salmon (use a baking sheet to help transfer if the piece is large) to a warm serving platter. Drizzle with Avocado Verde Sauce or serve the buerre blanc on the side.

Serves 15.

AVOCADO VERDE SAUCE

This dip is good drizzled on roasted or grilled salmon, served with vegetables, or as a salad dressing.

1½ cups verde sauce (page 52), or good quality sauce in a jar
½ poblano pepper, roasted, seeded and peeled
    (see note page 9)
1 avocado, peeled and sliced
juice of 1 lime
kosher salt and fresh ground black pepper to taste
dash of cayenne pepper if desired

Combine all of the ingredients in a blender. Purée until smooth. Adjust seasonings.

Makes about 1 pint.

ORZO WITH FRESH BASIL

2 pounds dry orzo pasta
3 tablespoons butter
1 cup extra virgin olive oil
8 cloves garlic, minced
½ teaspoon red pepper flakes
20 sun-dried tomato halves, soaked in warm water for 20
    minutes, drained, and chopped
¾ cup grated good-quality Parmesan cheese
basil purée to taste (see note page 9)
kosher salt and fresh ground black pepper to taste

In a large saucepan of boiling water, cook the orzo, 1 pound at a time, until tender (about 6 minutes for most brands). Meanwhile, in a sauté pan, melt the butter with the olive oil. Add the garlic, red pepper flakes, and sun-dried tomatoes and cook, stirring until fragrant, about 5 minutes. Toss the orzo with the oil mixture and add the basil. Add the Parmesan right before serving. Season to taste.

Serves 15 to 18.

ROASTED VEGETABLES

These vegetables are best cooked in a convection oven; they will be crisper and more caramelized. If you don't have convection, you can start the onions and peppers under the broiler to brown them. If you do use a convection oven, cut the cooking times by a third.

This dish is very forgiving and is good at room temperature. Leftovers are great on sandwiches with melted fresh mozzarella and basil leaves.

3 medium eggplants, cut into ½-inch pieces, salted, and left
    to drain in a colander for 30 minutes
2 red onions, cut into 1-1½ inch chunks
1 yellow onion, cut into 1-1½ inch chunks
1½ pounds carrots, peeled and cut into ½-inch thick pieces
    (or packaged baby-cut carrots)
12 medium new potatoes, cut into quarters lengthwise
3 red bell peppers, seeded and cut into triangular slices
3 green bell peppers, seeded and cut into triangular slices
12 medium Roma tomatoes, cut into 8 pieces
extra-virgin olive oil, about ¾ cup total
kosher salt and fresh ground black pepper

Heat the oven to 375°. In a large roasting pan, toss the new potatoes, onions, and carrots with about 3 tablespoons of olive oil and generous salt and pepper. Roast for about 15 minutes. Stir in the eggplants, peppers, and 3 to 4 more tablespoons of oil. Add a little more salt and pepper. After 15 more minutes, stir in the Roma tomatoes and more olive oil if the vegetables seem dry. Stir every 10 to 15 minutes, until the vegetables reach the desired tenderness, which usually takes about an hour. Season to taste.

Some good seasonal additions are: asparagus (added 10 to 15 minutes before you anticipate the vegetables will be ready) and butternut squash (peel and cut into ½-inch pieces, and add with the onions).

Serves about 15, or 18 to 20 with the addition of a medium butternut squash.

CRÈME BRÛLÉE

We adapted this recipe from an old Craig Claiborne cookbook. It's simple and fabulous. These custards set better and taste better if made the day before. They must be caramelized the day they are eaten, however, or the burnt sugar will start to weep.

For the custard:
8 cups heavy whipping cream
1 cup sugar
15 egg yolks from large eggs
1½ teaspoons pure vanilla extract

For the topping:
½ cup brown sugar
½ cup sugar

Preheat oven to 325°. In a medium heavy saucepan, heat the cream until hot to the touch. Add the sugar and stir to dissolve. Remove from heat. In a large bowl, whisk the egg yolks. Add the warm cream mixture to the eggs while whisking. Stir in the vanilla.

Place 16 (4-ounce) ramekins in a cake pan or roasting pan and pour enough warm water into the pan to reach halfway up the sides of the cups. Strain the mixture into a measuring cup with a pouring lip and fill the ramekins. Cover the entire pan with foil and bake until the custards are set, which is usually between 30 and 45 minutes, depending on the size and shape of the ramekins (see notes about custards, page 9). Meanwhile, mix the sugars for the topping and set aside.

Up to 4 hours before serving, spread a thin layer of the mixed sugars on the surfaces of the custards. Set custards on a baking sheet and broil (or torch—see below) the sugar on top to caramelize until it is brown and bubbly all over. Cool before serving.

For best results, caramelize the sugar with a small propane torch. Make sure the custards are on a metal surface with no fire hazards close by and remember not to touch the very hot ramekins after torching them.

SUMMER DINNER FOR 10

CRAB CAKES WITH SPICY REMOULADE
HERBED NEW POTATOES
SALAD WITH BALSAMIC-SOY-TAHINI DRESSING
CHOCOLATE WALNUT TART

This dinner can be done ahead entirely, but will yield better results if the crab cakes are fried right before serving. The new potatoes can be served room temperature or hot. For a compatible appetizer, try the Corn Tarts (about 2 dozen, page 19) or Pepper Cheese (page 13, about 1 pound). If you want to offer another vegetable, the Green Beans with Pistachios (page 78) are a good choice.

CRAB CAKES

These cakes are best made with fresh blue crab if possible (Dungeness in particular does not taste good in this recipe). I like to use the claw meat, but lump or back fin is also very good. For more flavor, substitute seasoned breadcrumbs, like those for the Tomato Stuffing (page 77), for about half of the toasted breadcrumbs in the coating.

16 green onions, white and green parts, chopped
dash Tabasco sauce
juice of 3 lemons
⅓ cup prepared mustard, Dijon or whole grain
4 teaspoons kosher salt
½ teaspoon white pepper
6 large eggs
4 cups fresh bread crumbs from French bread
2 pounds cooked blue crab meat, picked well for shell pieces
⅔ cup heavy cream
3 cups finely ground toasted breadcrumbs
oil for frying (safflower or canola)
1 recipe Spicy Remoulade
6 lemons, cut into wedges

In the bowl of the food processor, combine the green onions, Tabasco, lemon juice, mustard, salt, pepper, and eggs. Process until the onions are chopped fine. Transfer to a large bowl and mix with the fresh breadcrumbs, crabmeat, and cream. The mixture should be wet but dry enough to shape. If it's too dry, add a little more cream. If too wet, add a few breadcrumbs until the mixture will hold a compact shape. Form into cakes about 3 inches in diameter and ¾ inch thick. Gently toss in the toasted breadcrumbs to coat. Fry in about ½ inch of oil over medium high heat for about 3 minutes each side, until nut brown and crisp. Transfer to a pan lined with paper towels and keep warm in a 275° oven. Serve with Spicy Remoulade (following page) and lemon wedges.

Makes about 22 crab cakes.

SPICY REMOULADE

We used to check eggs carefully for cracks and keep them chilled until use to guard against salmonella. I have read that it actually occurs in only one in 10,000 eggs, but I can't vouch for current statistics. If you don't want to take the risk (which you should not if you have pregnant, elderly, or chronically ill guests) use pasteurized eggs or substitute good quality store-bought mayonnaise for the yolks, mustard, oils, and vinegar.

6 large egg yolks
3 tablespoons prepared mustard (Dijon or whole grain)
1 teaspoon white pepper
1½ teaspoons kosher salt
1 teaspoon black pepper
2 cups safflower or canola oil
½ cup olive oil
¼ cup red wine vinegar
3 cloves garlic, pressed
¼ cup capers
¼ cup green olives, chopped
juice of 2 limes
¼ teaspoon cayenne pepper

In the bowl of the food processor fitted with a steel blade, combine the egg yolks, mustard, salt and peppers. Process until the mixture is pale yellow, about 1 minute. Combine the oils in a measuring cup with a pouring lip. With machine running, pour in half of the oil mixture in a thin, steady stream. Add the vinegar, then drizzle in the remaining oils. Add the rest of the ingredients and process until the texture resembles tartar sauce. Adjust seasonings. For a creamier texture, add about 3 tablespoons warm water in the processor at the end.

Makes about 1 quart. Use leftover sauce for dipping roasted new potatoes or French fries.

HERBED NEW POTATOES

These potatoes are good hot or room temperature. If you have fresh tarragon, thyme, and dill, use twice the amounts called for. If you have other fresh herbs, you can substitute them, also in double quantities, for the ones named. Almost any herb will work well.

3 pounds new potatoes, scrubbed clean
2 tablespoons butter
⅓ cup olive oil
3 cloves garlic, minced
1 teaspoon dried dill leaves
1 teaspoon dried tarragon leaves
¼ teaspoon dried thyme leaves
½ teaspoon fresh basil purée (see note page 9)
⅛ teaspoon cayenne pepper
2 teaspoons kosher salt
fresh ground black pepper to taste
juice of ½ lemon

In a medium stockpot, cover the potatoes with cold water. Cook covered over high heat until a knife slides into the potatoes easily, about 30 minutes.

Meanwhile, melt the butter in a small sauté pan. Add the garlic, dill, tarragon, thyme, and basil, and stir over low heat until the garlic is cooked and the mixture is fragrant. Set aside.

When the potatoes are cooked, drain, cool just enough to handle, cut into quarters. While still warm, toss with the herb butter. Add cayenne, salt, pepper, and lemon juice to taste.

Makes about 10 servings.

BALSAMIC-SOY-TAHINI DRESSING

This dressing is great to have around. It will keep in a clean jar in the refrigerator for at least 2 weeks. Serve it on salads, asparagus, or sugar snap peas. A little goes a long way. Since green vegetables will start to weep once mixed with the dressing, toss them just before serving.

1 cup balsamic vinegar
1 cup good quality soy sauce
¾ cup canola or safflower oil
1 cup tahini (sesame paste)
4 to 6 medium garlic cloves, minced

Combine all the ingredients and blend until smooth. Makes about 3 cups.

SALAD FOR 10

1 large head red romaine lettuce, washed well and spun dry
1 head red leaf lettuce, washed well and spun dry
6 carrots, peeled
10 Roma tomatoes, cut into wedges
1 cup toasted sliced almonds

Cut or tear the lettuce into bite-size pieces. Make carrot ribbons by pressing hard with a peeler over the length of the carrot. To serve, toss everything except almonds together with about ½ cup dressing, adding more to taste. Sprinkle almonds on top.

CHOCOLATE WALNUT TART

I once flew to Boston for Thanksgiving with this tart in my book bag. I had chilled it and wrapped the entire thing in plastic. It fared beautifully. This tart slices and tastes best at room temperature.

¼ cup butter, melted
½ cup honey
½ cup packed brown sugar
1 teaspoon vanilla
2 large eggs
½ teaspoon kosher salt
2 cups (or more) walnut pieces
5 ounces semisweet chocolate, melted

unbaked Short Crust Pastry (page 30) cut, pressed into a
    10-inch scalloped tart pan, and pricked almost through
    with a fork every 2 inches

Preheat the oven to 350°. In a medium bowl, combine the butter, honey, brown sugar, vanilla, eggs, and salt. Mix well. Stir in 2 cups walnut pieces and pour into prepared tart shell. If the mixture does not quite fill the shell evenly, gently stir in a few more walnuts, being careful not to damage the crust. Bake for 20 to 25 minutes, until the walnuts are lightly toasted and the filling is set. When cool, top with the melted chocolate. Chill slightly until the chocolate is firm.

Serves 8 to 10.

SQUARE SHOULDER OF LAMB

...ed and well trimmed the square shoulder, brush...
...th melted butter, and grill it gently.
...lmost cooked, sprinkle it again with melted but...
...ubs, and let it acquire a golden brown tint wit...
...eking it.

...hot with mint sauce (136) and a suitable garnish.

EELLE SQUARE SHOULDER OF LAMB   Carré d'Agneau Printani...

...n potatoes (2203) in an oval earthenware dish...
...rity of potatoes of raw, minced artichoke...

PAELLA DINNER FOR 20

PAELLA WITH CHICKEN AND SEAFOOD
GREEN BEANS WITH FENNEL AND RADICCHIO
ORANGE FLAN

This menu is easy to serve. Many of the items may be done ahead and require little attention once on the table.

You can set aside a couple of portions of paella before adding the seafood if you think you might have guests who don't eat it.

If you want to simplify, serve pick-up desserts, such as lemon tarts, brownies, or white chocolate oat bars instead of flan. By eliminating the custards, you save the last-minute step of removing them from the cups and you have fewer dishes and spoons to wash later.

For appetizers, consider Spanish cheeses and olives or the Ancho Torta (page 26) with crackers.

PAELLA WITH CHICKEN AND SEAFOOD

Don't let the ingredient list scare you. This is a great dish for entertaining for a couple of reasons: it is easily adaptable to your favorite seafood and it doesn't have to be kept piping hot to be delicious. The chicken and seafood may be prepared while the rice cooks. Add Spanish chorizo if you wish.

1 cup dry white wine
pinch (½ to ¾ teaspoon) saffron threads
¼ cup olive oil
2 large yellow onions, sliced
1 head of garlic (about 10 cloves), peeled and minced fine
1 teaspoon red pepper flakes
6 bell peppers, red, green or mixed, sliced
20 Roma tomatoes, quartered
10 cups chicken stock
6 cups uncooked rice (white, Basmati, or other)
about 4 cups cooked chicken, sliced
2 pounds medium shrimp, peeled, cleaned, and sautéed
    in 3 tablespoons olive oil with 2 cloves minced garlic
    until barely firm
1 pound squid, scallops or mussels, poached in white wine
    or water for about 3 minutes
10-ounce package frozen green peas
about 2 teaspoons Hungarian paprika
kosher salt and black pepper, to taste
juice of 3 lemons or limes, as needed

Gently heat the white wine with the saffron and set aside to steep.

Meanwhile, in a large roasting pan, sauté the onions, garlic, red pepper flakes, and bell peppers in olive oil over medium heat until soft. Add the tomatoes and cook 5 more minutes. Add the rice and sauté for another 2 minutes. Pour in the chicken stock and the wine with saffron. Bring to a boil, then stir and reduce heat to a simmer. Cover and cook over medium heat.

While the rice cooks, prepare the chicken and seafood. Check rice for doneness after 12 minutes. Add the peas and let sit for 3 to 4 minutes. Stir in seafood, chicken, paprika, salt, and pepper. Mix well. Add lemon or lime juice to taste.

You can prepare the dish ahead, up to the point of adding the rice. If you are less than confident about cooking rice, use the converted kind. It is almost foolproof, but you sacrifice the flavor that other rice takes on.

Serves 18 to 22.

GREEN BEANS WITH MARINATED FENNEL AND RADICCHIO

If you need to make this ahead of time, be sure to toss everything together right before serving. Mixing the dressing with the beans too far ahead of time will turn them army drab.

1 medium fennel bulb, sliced thin
¼ cup balsamic vinegar
2 tablespoons olive oil

3½ to 4 pounds green beans, preferably harvesters or
    haricots verts, ends trimmed
1 head radicchio, trimmed of core and sliced

For the dressing:
½ cup olive oil
3 tablespoons balsamic vinegar
1 teaspoon Dijon mustard
kosher salt and fresh ground black pepper to taste

Marinate the fennel in the vinegar and olive oil. Set aside for at least 10 minutes. For best flavor, marinate the fennel overnight.

Cook the green beans in boiling water for 6 minutes (4 minutes for haricots). Taste to check (they should be still crisp but not woody tasting) and cook for longer if necessary. Drain, cool in ice water and drain, letting sit until dry.

Whisk together the dressing ingredients and combine ⅓ cup (add more if needed) with the green beans, marinated fennel, and radicchio immediately before serving. Toss only what you'll need, as the beans lose their color and flavor just a few hours after they are combined with the dressing.

Serves 20.

ORANGE FLAN

This flan is easier to deal with if it is made a day ahead. Each cup will yield more caramel syrup if it has sat overnight. I recommend making this silky custard in small cups (4 to 6-ounce) rather than in one large dish. The flan is soft, not dense, and is prone to disaster when turned out from a large dish.

For the caramel:
2 cups sugar
1 cup water

For the custard:
1 orange, washed well
2 sugar cubes (optional, see below)
1⅓ cups milk
1⅓ cups heavy cream
1 cinnamon stick
1 teaspoon vanilla extract
1 tablespoon liqueur (brandy, rum, or Cointreau)
5 large eggs
6 additional egg yolks
1 cup sugar

To make the caramel, combine the sugar and water in a small heavy saucepan. Bring to a boil and cook until nut brown. Remove from heat and pour ¼ inch deep into each custard cup (you will probably have caramel left over). Place prepared cups in a roasting pan and pour enough warm water to reach halfway up the sides of the cups. Set aside.

Preheat oven to 350°. Use the sugar cubes to chafe the surface of the orange, removing its zest and oils. Place zest and sugar cubes in a medium saucepan. If you prefer, you can use a zester or peeler to remove only the orange zest (avoid the bitter white pith). Chop very fine. Add the milk, cream, and cinnamon stick to the saucepan and heat until bubbles form around the edge of the pan, until the mixture is hot. Remove from heat. Add the vanilla and the liqueur. Set aside to cool.

Meanwhile, whisk the eggs and yolks together until pale. Add the sugar slowly, mixing well. Strain the milk mixture into the egg mixture and whisk together. Strain into cups, cover, and bake until the custard is firm, but not stiff, 45 minutes to an hour. If you need to speed up cooking, remove the cover for the last few minutes of baking. Cool to room temperature before refrigerating until serving. To remove the custards from the cups, run a knife around the sides of the dishes and carefully invert onto the serving plates.

Makes 20 small (4-ounce) cups.

fORK & KNIFE fOOD

BEEF TENDERLOIN DINNER FOR 12

DUXELLES TENDERLOIN
HERB-STUFFED TOMATO HALVES
BASMATI RICE WITH DRIED FIGS AND HAZELNUTS
GREEN BEANS WITH PISTACHIOS
CHOCOLATE FLAN

This is a hearty menu, which is best served hot. The green beans could be done ahead and reheated in the microwave, but the tenderloin, tomato halves, and rice require some last-minute attention.

DUXELLES TENDERLOIN

For the tenderloin:
6 tablespoons butter
4 medium shallots, chopped
1 pound white or cremini mushrooms, chopped
fresh nutmeg
kosher salt and fresh ground pepper to taste
2 tablespoons dry sherry
whole beef tenderloin, trimmed, about 5 pounds

For the sauce:
1 tablespoon butter
3 sliced shallots
½ pound chopped mushrooms, assorted varieties
2 to 3 cups beef stock
½ cup red wine
4 Roma tomatoes, minced
2 teaspoons dried tarragon
kosher salt and fresh ground black pepper to taste

To make the duxelles, melt 3 tablespoons of butter over medium heat in a sauté pan and add the shallots and mushrooms. When the moisture from the mushrooms has evaporated, add the seasonings and sherry and stir briefly over low heat.

Slice almost through the tenderloin lengthwise, leaving about ½-inch uncut at the bottom. Make shallow lengthwise incisions on either side of the first cut to feather the meat, making it flatter and of even thickness. Spread the duxelles on this flat surface and roll the meat around the filling, into a long, even roll. Tie with trussing string every 2 inches or seal with toothpicks or skewers. If you want to work ahead, you may refrigerate the tenderloin at this point until later use.

Preheat oven to 375°. In a large metal roasting pan, melt the remaining butter over medium heat. Brown the beef on each side. Roast 20 minutes for medium rare. While the tenderloin cooks, start the sauce as instructed below. When the beef is cooked to your taste, remove from pan and set aside to rest for about 10 minutes. Slice into ¾-inch portions and serve on a warm platter.

To make the sauce, melt the butter over medium heat in a saucepan and add the shallots. Add the mushrooms and sauté until tender. Add 2 cups beef stock, red wine, tomatoes, and tarragon and bring to a boil. Season well with salt and pepper and continue to boil. Add wine and stock to taste and continue to boil until the sauce has reduced by half. After the tenderloin is removed from the oven, add the sauce to the pan drippings and adjust the seasonings.

Serves 12.

HERB-STUFFED TOMATO HALVES

Stuffed tomatoes were always on our menu. This stuffing also makes a great substitute for plain breadcrumbs. It is particularly good as a coating on the crab cakes (page 64). The olive oil moistens the mixture a little, but it re-crisps when toasted. If you like, try adding feta cheese or Parmesan when stuffing tomatoes.

For the stuffing:
5 cups breadcrumbs made from sliced and toasted day-old
    French bread
½ cup olive oil
6 cloves garlic, minced
6 shallots, peeled and cut into ½-inch pieces
2½ teaspoons kosher salt
2 tablespoons black pepper
2 teaspoons thyme
2 tablespoons fresh basil purée (see note page 9)

8 whole beefsteak tomatoes

In a food processor, grind the breadcrumbs with the steel blade until fine. Pour the crumbs into a medium bowl. Combine the rest of the stuffing ingredients in the processor and pulse until smooth. Add the breadcrumbs to this mixture and mix well. Add more breadcrumbs if the mixture appears wet rather than moist.

Preheat oven to 375°. To stuff the tomatoes, cut each tomato in half through the "equator" and cut out the core. Poke your fingers into the seed cavities to remove the seeds and squeeze out the liquid. Fill the cavities with stuffing and firmly pack the tomato half, slightly mounding the top. Bake until light brown, about 10 to 15 minutes. You may also be brown the tomatoes under the broiler.

Makes about 6 cups of stuffing, enough for about 18 tomato halves. Store leftover crumbs in an airtight container. They will keep for 2 weeks in the refrigerator, longer in the freezer.

BASMATI RICE WITH DRIED FIGS AND HAZELNUTS

1 cup hazelnuts
3 tablespoons butter
1 medium yellow onion, chopped (about I cup)
2 cups Basmati rice
4 cups chicken stock
1½ cups water
2 tablespoons sherry or white wine
1 cup chopped dried figs
2 teaspoons brown sugar
1 teaspoon kosher salt
fresh black pepper to taste

Toast the hazelnuts in a 300° oven until the skins start to split and the nuts are starting to brown slightly. Cool a few minutes. Rub between hands to remove most of the skins. Chop coarsely and set aside.

In a large saucepan, melt the butter over medium heat. Add the onion and sauté until soft. Add the rice and stir over medium heat for about 1 minute. Add the chicken stock, water, wine, figs, and brown sugar. Bring to a boil. Reduce to a simmer. Cover and cook 20 to 25 minutes, until the grains are tender. Let sit covered for 3 to 4 minutes. Stir in hazelnuts and season with salt and pepper to taste.

Serves 12.

GREEN BEANS WITH PISTACHIOS

These beans may be made with any good fresh green bean (I prefer harvesters or haricots verts). If using haricots (French green beans), check the beans after 4 minutes of cooking. There are also a couple of tasty brands of frozen haricots verts that you could quickly sauté in the butter then toss with the pistachios.

about 2 pounds green beans, trimmed of ends
3 to 4 tablespoons melted butter
about ¼ cup ground pistachio nuts, more if desired
kosher salt and fresh black pepper

Bring about 4 quarts of water in a stockpot to a boil. Add the beans and cook until crisp-tender and still bright green, about 6 minutes. Drain until dry and toss with melted butter until well coated. Sprinkle with ground pistachios and season well with salt and pepper. If making the beans ahead of time, cool them in ice water immediately after cooking to preserve their color. Before serving, toss first with the butter and then the nuts.

Serves about 12.

CHOCOLATE FLAN

You will need 14 (3 to 4-ounce) custard cups, or ramekins, for this recipe. As I've mentioned elsewhere, cooking time for custards can vary wildly—even in the same oven. This recipe is best made the day before so that the flans will set up and be easier to remove from the dishes.

For the caramel:
2 ½ cups sugar
1 ¼ cups water

For the custard:
3 cups heavy cream
1 ½ cups milk
1 cup plus 2 tablespoons sugar
5 ounces good quality bittersweet chocolate, melted
3 large eggs
6 additional egg yolks
1 ½ teaspoons vanilla extract
¼ teaspoon ground cinnamon

Place the ramekins in a large baking pan and pour enough warm water into the pan to reach halfway up the sides of the cups. Set aside.

To make the caramel, combine the sugar and water in a heavy saucepan and cook over high heat until the mixture starts to brown. It will take several minutes, but will brown quickly once it starts to take on color. Working quickly, pour about ¼ inch of caramel into the bottom of each prepared cup. Set aside.

In a large saucepan, combine the cream, milk, and sugar and cook over medium heat until sugar melts. Add the chocolate and whisk until smooth. Remove from heat.

Preheat oven to 350°. In a large bowl, whisk the eggs, yolks, vanilla, and cinnamon. While continuing to whisk, add the warm chocolate mixture slowly to the egg mixture. Pour the custard into the prepared cups and cover the pan with foil. Bake until set, about 40 minutes. Refrigerate. To serve, run a knife around the inside of the cup and invert onto a plate.

Makes about 14 individual flans.

DO-AHEAD LUNCH FOR 12

ORANGE-MARINATED GAME HENS
PEANUT NOODLES
BROCCOLI WITH HONEY MUSTARD DRESSING
LIME-MACADAMIA BARS

All of the items on this menu taste good at room temperature. For bread, I would recommend something eggy, such as challah. If you want to add something else, consider Rosario's Black Beans (page 54).

ORANGE-MARINATED GAME HENS

You must allow several hours for these hens to marinate, but they're worth it.

For the marinade:
2 tablespoons grainy mustard
⅓ cup soy sauce
1 large shallot, cut into pieces
3 cloves garlic, minced
¼ cup safflower or canola oil
2-inch piece fresh ginger root, peeled and sliced thin
¼ cup dry sherry
zest and juice of 3 oranges

6 to 8 Cornish game hens, cut in half through the breast
    and backbones
¼ cup honey

Combine the marinade ingredients in a blender. Purée until smooth. In a large bowl, toss game hen halves in marinade until well coated. Marinate several hours or overnight.

To roast, preheat oven to 400°. Arrange hen halves spaced apart on a shallow foil-lined roasting pan. Reserve marinade. Roast until their juices run clear when you insert a knifepoint at the thigh, 25 to 35 minutes.

Meanwhile, pour reserved marinade into a small heavy saucepan and add honey. Reduce over medium heat until thick and syrupy. Baste hen halves halfway through cooking and again when they are removed from the oven.

Serve hot or at room temperature.

Serves 10 to 12.

PEANUT NOODLES

These noodles are a great picnic dish. They keep well, taste great, and will suit vegans if made with egg-free pasta. For crowds I don't know, I often make this recipe with cashews rather than peanuts—there seem to be fewer people allergic to cashews.

1 pound dry capellini noodles, cooked according to
    directions on package
½ cup toasted sesame oil, divided
12 green onions, green and white parts, minced
4 cloves garlic, minced
½ teaspoon red pepper flakes
2 tablespoons rice wine vinegar
2 teaspoons sugar
¼ cup soy sauce
1 cup chopped roasted peanuts
⅓ cup chopped cilantro leaves (no stems)
kosher salt and fresh ground black pepper to taste

In a large bowl, toss the cooked pasta with ¼ cup sesame oil. Set aside.

In a small sauté pan, heat remaining sesame oil. Add the green onions, garlic, and red pepper flakes. Stir over medium heat until the green onions are slightly soft and the mixture is fragrant.

To the green onion mixture, stir in the rice wine vinegar, sugar, and soy sauce. Toss with the noodles. Add the nuts and cilantro and season to taste.

Serve cold or room temperature.

Serves 12.

BROCCOLI WITH HONEY MUSTARD DRESSING

We made this dressing by the gallon at Lilly & Co. and probably used enough over the years to fill a swimming pool. It's strong and addictive stuff.

About 3 bunches broccoli (12 large spears)

For the dressing:
4 cloves garlic, minced
¾ cup coarse mustard
⅓ cup honey
¼ cup soy sauce

Cut and trim the broccoli into serving-sized pieces (I like the floret with an inch of stem). Cook in boiling water for 4 minutes. Plunge into ice water. Drain well.

Whisk the dressing ingredients together in a medium bowl. Drizzle desired amount of dressing over broccoli before serving. Start with a little and add to taste.

The broccoli will keep for a couple of days if undressed. The dressing will keep for a couple of weeks, refrigerated in a covered jar.

Serves 10 to 12.

LIME - MACADAMIA BARS

For the pastry:
2 sticks (½ pound) butter, cut into ½-inch pieces
2 cups all-purpose flour
⅔ cup powdered sugar
¾ cup chopped macadamia nuts (about 3 ounces)
1 teaspoon grated lime zest (save another teaspoon
    for the custard)
¼ teaspoon kosher salt

For the custard topping:
4 large eggs
1½ cups sugar
¾ cups lime juice, from 6 to 8 medium limes
1 teaspoon baking powder
¼ cup all-purpose flour
1 teaspoon grated lime zest
½ cup unsweetened coconut flakes (optional)

Preheat oven to 350°. In a processor bowl, combine the pastry ingredients and pulse until well mixed. It will seem dry. Press into a greased 9 X 13-inch cake pan, forming a small lip around the sides. Bake until golden brown, about 13 to 16 minutes.

To make the custard, whisk the eggs and sugar well in a medium bowl. Stir in the rest of the ingredients except the coconut and pour over the warm pastry. Sprinkle the coconut over the top. Bake 12 to 16 minutes, until the top is golden and the custard is set.

Cool and cut into 24 bars. Refrigerate.

SUNDAY SUPPER FOR 8

SPICE-RUBBED PORK TENDERLOIN
WILD RICE WITH MANGOS AND PECANS
BABY SPINACH WITH BALSAMIC DRESSING
FRUIT CRISP

This dinner is easy and could be prepared ahead and served at
room temperature. If you want to add another vegetable, try
the Cherry Tomatoes with Feta and Mint (page 37). A good fruit
chutney works well with the pork.

SPICE-RUBBED PORK TENDERLOIN

This spice rub is great on salmon, too. I make gallons of it each year for teacher and host gifts, as well as for my personal addiction. Though you will have some left over if you make the amount below, I would recommend making double and saving some for later.

For the rub:
1 cup light brown sugar
4 teaspoons chile powder (I like New Mexico mixed with a little chipotle powder)
4 teaspoons kosher salt
½ teaspoon black pepper
⅛ teaspoon cloves
⅛ teaspoon cumin ·
1 teaspoon cayenne

4 pounds pork tenderloin, trimmed of fat

Preheat the oven to 375°. Mix the rub ingredients together in a small bowl. Spread about ¼ cup over the pork tenderloins and rub into the meat, coating all sides well. Add more as necessary. On a foil-lined baking pan, roast the pork until the interior temperature is 150° (see below), 20 to 30 minutes. Let the pork sit for a few minutes before slicing. Pour the syrupy pan drippings over the sliced pork and serve warm or at room temperature.

Makes 8 to 10 servings.

Note: I have read in the last few years that pink pork is considered safe, especially if it has been frozen for 20 days. To cook it too much is to dry it out and destroy the flavor. If you prefer, the pork may also be grilled or smoked and the same temperature rules apply.

WILD RICE WITH MANGOS AND PECANS

The bright lemon and mango are nice flavor and color contrasts to the earthy wild rice.

1¼ pounds uncooked wild rice
3 tablespoons butter
1 small yellow onion, chopped
2 medium mangos, peeled and cut into ½-inch pieces
zest and juice of 1 lemon
¾ cup chopped pecans, toasted
kosher salt and fresh ground black pepper to taste

Rinse the wild rice. In a large saucepan, cover the rice with twice as much water. Bring to a boil. Reduce to a simmer and cover, adding more water as needed. Check for doneness after about 25 minutes. The grains should have burst slightly but should not be gummy. Drain if necessary.

While the rice cooks, melt the butter in a sauté pan. Sauté the onion until soft. Add the mango and continue to cook until the mango is warmed through, or if the mango is slightly unripe, cook it until sweet. Toss with the cooked wild rice. Add the lemon and pecans and season to taste. Serve warm or room temperature.

Serves 8 to 10.

BABY SPINACH WITH BALSAMIC VINAIGRETTE

For the dressing:
¼ cup balsamic vinegar
⅔ cup olive oil, or a mixture of canola oil and olive oil
1 tablespoon Dijon mustard or grainy mustard
½ teaspoon kosher salt
fresh ground black pepper to taste

1½ pounds baby spinach leaves, trimmed of any large stems and washed
2 red or orange bell peppers, roasted (see note page 9), peeled, and sliced
2 avocados, peeled and sliced
¼ cup red onion, sliced paper-thin
1 head radicchio, cored and sliced thin

Combine the dressing ingredients and mix well. If too sharp to the taste, add a little mustard, oil, or salt. If too oily, add a little vinegar or salt.

Combine the salad ingredients in a large serving bowl and toss with the dressing immediately before serving, adding only half at first, more if needed.

Makes 8 to 10 servings.

FRUIT CRISP

The minute the first berries hit the farmer's market in the spring, I load up and go straight home to make this crisp. I like it simple and unadulterated, but you could always add pecans or almonds to the topping. This recipe does not double well; for a large crowd, make two separate small pans.

9 cups fresh fruit (one or more of the following: stemmed and halved strawberries, blackberries, raspberries, peeled and sliced peaches)
1⅓ cups packed light brown sugar
1 cup all-purpose flour
1 cup quick-cooking oats
1 stick (¼ pound) butter, cut small

Preheat oven to 375°. Place the cut-up fruit in a baking pan, preferably ceramic, ideally about 8 X 12 inches. The fruit should fill the pan. Mix the rest of the ingredients together and sprinkle evenly on the top. Bake until the fruit is bubbly and the top has started to brown, 20 to 30 minutes. Serve with cream, plain or whipped, or ice cream.

Serves 8.

EASY DINNER FOR 8

BEEF TENDERLOIN WITH CALAMATA RUB
ROMAINE SALAD WITH LEMON DRESSING
ORZO WITH SPINACH AND PINE NUTS
CLASSIC CHEESECAKE

This dinner is no-fuss. If you need appetizers, keep it easy with figs, Italian cheeses, grapes, almonds, and anything else you can just unwrap and plop in a serving piece.

BEEF TENDERLOIN WITH CALAMATA RUB

For the rub:
1 cup pitted Calamata olives
2 medium shallots, coarsely chopped
7 cloves garlic, minced
juice of 1 lemon
2 tablespoons basil purée (see note, page 9)
¼ cup olive oil

4 pounds beef tenderloin, trimmed of fat

Combine all rub ingredients in food processor and purée into a paste. Add more oil if necessary.

Preheat oven to 375°. Rub the outside of the beef tenderloin with the Calamata mixture, patting on as much as possible. In a roasting pan, roast the tenderloin until cooked to your liking, 30 to 40 minutes for medium rare. Let sit for about 10 minutes before slicing. Serve warm or at room temperature.

Serves 8 to 10.

ROMAINE SALAD WITH LEMON DRESSING

For the dressing:
zest and juice of 1 lemon
3 tablespoons raspberry vinegar
1 clove garlic, minced
¾ cup canola or safflower oil
¼ cup olive oil
1 teaspoon Dijon mustard, more if desired
kosher salt and fresh ground black pepper to taste

2 heads romaine lettuce, washed and cut into bite-sized pieces
optional: grated Parmesan cheese, roasted peppers (see page 9), tomato wedges, carrots, croutons, etc.

Combine all dressing ingredients and mix well. If dressing tastes too sharp, add salt or mustard. If too oily, add more lemon juice.

Toss ½ cup dressing with the lettuce, adding more as needed. Mix in any optional ingredients.

Serves 8.

ORZO PASTA WITH SPINACH AND PINE NUTS

¼ cup olive oil, more if needed
1 yellow onion, chopped
3 cloves garlic, minced
2 portabella mushrooms, sliced and cut into ½-inch pieces
10 sun-dried tomato halves, plumped in hot water, or packed
    in oil, chopped
1½ pounds orzo pasta, cooked according to package
    instructions
12 ounces fresh spinach, stemmed, washed, wilted over
    low heat, drained well, and chopped
¾ cup pine nuts, toasted at 300° for about 4 minutes
½ to ¾ cup grated Parmesan or Romano cheese
kosher salt and fresh ground black pepper to taste

In a medium sauté pan, combine the olive oil, onion, garlic, and mushrooms. Cook over medium heat until the onions are translucent. Add the sun-dried tomatoes and cook for about 2 minutes more. Toss the mushroom mixture with the cooked pasta. Add the spinach, pine nuts and mix well, adding more oil if necessary. Stir in the cheese.

Note: too much Parmesan will turn the pasta gummy. Serve warm or room temperature.

Makes 8 to 12 servings.

CLASSIC CHEESECAKE

For the crust:
1¼ cups graham cracker crumbs
2 tablespoons sugar
¼ teaspoon freshly grated nutmeg

For the cheesecake:
2 pounds cream cheese (or Neufchâtel cheese),
    room temperature
1½ cups sugar
1 cup plus 2 tablespoons sour cream
1 teaspoon vanilla extract
zest of 1 lemon
2 teaspoons lemon juice
4 large eggs

Butter the sides of a 10-inch springform pan. Preheat the oven to 350°. Combine the crust ingredients and pour them into the pan. Tilt the pan to coat the sides evenly with crumbs then tap the pan to evenly distribute the rest of the crumbs on the bottom for the crust. Set aside.

In a large mixing bowl, cream the cheese until soft and fluffy, scraping the paddle and sides of the bowl as needed. Add the sugar and mix well. Add the sour cream, vanilla, and lemon zest and juice. Add the eggs 1 at a time, mixing as little as possible. Pour into the prepared pan and place in a larger pan. Pour about an inch of water in the larger pan. Bake until the sides have puffed up a little and the middle of the cake wobbles like jelly. Insert a knife into the middle of the cheesecake. It should come out clean or lightly beaded, but not milky. Cool slowly, at room temperature for an hour, before refrigerating. This cheesecake needs to be refrigerated for about two hours before it is sliced.

Note: the cheesecake may crack if the eggs are beaten too long or if the cheesecake is cooled too quickly.

Serves 12.

COMFORT FOOD DINNER FOR 8

ROASTED CHICKEN BREASTS WITH RED WINE, TOMATO, AND BACON SAUCE
CREAMY POLENTA WITH ASIAGO AND SPINACH LEAVES
CHOPPED SALAD WITH RADICCHIO
UPSIDE-DOWN PEAR GINGERBREAD

This menu is pure comfort, with a little nod to health. After this dinner you will be able to walk against the wind, as a very tiny elderly friend used to say.

ROASTED CHICKEN BREASTS WITH RED WINE, TOMATO, AND BACON SAUCE

This dish requires a little bit of attention to timing, as the tomato sauce needs a head start. Have the chicken breasts wait patiently while the sauce finishes cooking. Assembly is a snap if everything is ready to go.

5 slices bacon
4 tablespoons olive oil, divided
3 medium shallots, sliced
3 cloves garlic, minced
1 (25-ounce) can chopped tomatoes
2 large tomatoes, chopped
1 cup dry red wine
2 teaspoons kosher salt
fresh black pepper to taste
½ pound mushrooms, sliced
1 teaspoon sugar, if needed for balance
12 boneless, skin-on chicken breast halves
3 tablespoons chopped fresh basil leaves, for garnish

about 6 packed cups sliced fresh spinach leaves,
    stems trimmed and washed well

In a large sauté pan, fry the bacon over medium heat until barely cooked (not crisp). Remove from heat and drain on paper towels. Chop and set aside. Pour off all but 1 tablespoon of the bacon grease and return the pan to medium heat. Add 2 tablespoons of the olive oil, shallots, and garlic and sauté for about 2 minutes. Add both tomatoes and red wine and simmer for about 20 minutes. Add the salt, pepper, and mushrooms and simmer for another 30 minutes, until the flavors have blended. Add sugar if the sauce tastes tinny.

Preheat the oven to 375°. Prepare a large roasting pan with cooking spray and set aside. Heat the remaining olive oil in a large sauté pan over medium heat. Brown the chicken breasts, skin side first, for about 2 minutes per side. Transfer to a roasting pan and salt and pepper well. Roast for 10 to 15 minutes, until the surface of the meat springs back when touched and the interior temperature reaches 160°. While the chicken cooks, make the polenta (recipe follows).

To serve, spoon polenta onto warmed plates. Cover with spinach leaves. Arrange the chicken breasts on the spinach and dress with warm tomato sauce. Garnish with chopped basil and Asiago cheese, as described on the following page.

Serves 8.

CREAMY POLENTA WITH ASIAGO

To serve the polenta soft, as with the roasted chicken, timing is important. It needs to be served immediately after cooking.

You can make firm polenta ahead. Prepare 2 (8 X 8-inch) roasting pans with non-stick cooking spray and a layer of waxed paper. Pour cooked polenta into pans, smooth top with a buttered spatula, cover, and refrigerate. To serve, warm the polenta in the pan (about 25 minutes at 300°) and cut into squares. Or, first cut the chilled polenta into pieces and grill or griddle them to heat them through.

8 cups milk
4 tablespoons butter, cut into ½-inch pieces
2 teaspoons kosher salt
fresh ground black pepper
2½ cups quick-cooking polenta
1½ cups grated Asiago cheese, plus more for garnish

In a large heavy saucepan, combine the milk, butter, salt, and pepper. Warm over medium heat until the butter is melted. Slowly add the polenta stirring continuously. Cook, scraping the bottom and sides well, until the mixture thickens, about 8 minutes (check package for cooking times). Off heat, stir in the Asiago. Serve immediately.

Serves 8.

CHOPPED SALAD WITH RADICCHIO

This salad welcomes different additions. Try adding cubed feta, fresh herbs, avocado, or toasted pistachios just before tossing to serve. Sturdier ingredients such as cherry tomatoes or cooked fresh corn could be added any time.

½ cup chopped radicchio, core discarded
1 cup peeled and chopped carrots
2 medium zucchini, chopped
1 hothouse cucumber, peeled, seeded, and chopped
3 bell peppers, various colors, seeded, and chopped
3 medium chopped new potatoes, cooked in boiling water
    until barely tender
3 tablespoons olive oil
3 to 4 tablespoons fruity vinegar (fig infused balsamic is
    my favorite)
juice of 1 lemon
kosher salt and fresh ground black pepper

In a medium bowl, combine all ingredients and adjust the seasonings, if necessary.

Serves 8 to 10.

UPSIDE-DOWN PEAR GINGERBREAD

This recipe is adapted from one I discovered in England while attending London's Cordon Bleu. This cake is dark and rich, fabulous with sour cream or plain yogurt. It serves 12, but is easily halved. A half recipe can be baked in a 9-inch round cake pan.

For the bottom of the pan:
1 stick (¼ pound) butter
½ cup packed light brown sugar
3 pears, slightly under ripe, peeled and sliced

For the batter:
2 sticks (½ pound) butter
2 cups packed light brown sugar
4 large eggs
1 cup molasses
3½ cups all-purpose flour
2 teaspoons baking soda
1 teaspoon salt
2 tablespoons ground cinnamon
1 tablespoon ground ginger
1 teaspoon fresh ground nutmeg
2 cups milk
sour cream or plain yogurt for garnish, optional

Preheat the oven to 375°. Spray the bottom and sides of a 9 X 13 X 2-inch pan with non-stick cooking spray. In a medium mixing bowl, cream the butter and brown sugar until fluffy. Spread evenly on the bottom of the prepared pan and arrange the pear slices, pressing them into the sugar mixture. Set aside.

To make the batter, beat the butter and brown sugar in a medium bowl. Add the eggs 1 at a time, scraping the side of the bowl between each addition. Add the molasses. Sift together the flour, baking soda, salt, and spices. Add the dry ingredients alternately with the milk. Pour the batter over the pears. Place the pan on a sheet tray, to catch sticky drips, and bake for about 35 minutes, until a toothpick inserted in the middle of the pan (but not as deep as the brown sugar-pear layer) comes out clean. Turn out while still warm by running a knife around the edge of the pan and centering the serving platter over the cake. Holding the sides of both the pan and the platter, carefully flip, and lift the pan off. Serve with sour cream or yogurt on the side.

Serves 12.

SHRIMP PICNIC DINNER FOR 4-6

SHRIMP WITH HERBED COCONUT MILK RICE
ASPARAGUS WITH SESAME DRESSING
NUT BUTTER COOKIES

This menu is very easy to prepare ahead of time. If it's summer and you have great homegrown tomatoes, slice them, sprinkle with kosher salt or sea salt and serve them separately from the rice.

SHRIMP WITH HERBED COCONUT MILK RICE

I used to make this recipe with a smaller quantity of herbs. I liked their subtlety and freshness. When we updated our recipe (or perhaps finally wrote it down), we beefed up the herbs and suddenly perked up to new possibilities with this dish. Serve it mild (go easy on the herbs) or spicy (add another serrano), warm or cold; it will whisper or shout the arrival of spring. If you can't get good fresh serrano peppers, you may use a jalapeño pepper instead. Delicious served warm or cold.

1 (13.5-ounce) can coconut milk or "lite" coconut milk
⅓ cup cilantro leaves
⅓ cup fresh mint leaves
⅓ cup fresh basil leaves (any variety of basil is good)
1 serrano pepper, seeded
2 teaspoons kosher salt, divided
½ teaspoon sugar
2 cups Texmati or other fragrant white rice
3½ cups water
2 pounds medium (21 to 25 count) shrimp, peeled and
    cleaned, kept ice cold
¼ cup red onion, sliced thin
1 large tomato, cut into ½-inch pieces
1 cucumber, peeled and seeded, sliced thin

In a blender or processor bowl, combine the coconut milk, herbs, serrano pepper, 1 teaspoon salt, and sugar. Purée until smooth.

Pour about ¾ cup of the coconut milk mixture into a large saucepan. Add the rice, water and remaining salt. Bring to a boil. Reduce to a simmer and cover. Cook for 10 to 12 minutes, until just tender. Remove from heat and let sit for 3 or 4 minutes, covered, to continue steaming.

Meanwhile, preheat oven to 350°. Toss the shrimp with all of the remaining marinade—it will look like a lot—and arrange them in rows in a shallow roasting pan. Bake for about 8 minutes, until the shrimp is opaque and springs back when touched.

To serve, stir the red onion, tomato, and cucumber into the warm rice and adjust the seasonings. Spoon onto plates and arrange the shrimp (with their sauce from the pan) on top.

Serves 4 to 6.

ASPARAGUS WITH SESAME DRESSING

¼ cup toasted sesame oil
1 clove garlic, minced
About 1½ pounds fresh asparagus, trimmed and cut at
    an angle into 2-inch pieces
2 tablespoons soy sauce
1 tablespoon rice wine vinegar
2 tablespoons toasted sesame seeds

In a large non-reactive skillet, warm the sesame oil over medium heat. Add the garlic and sauté for about 1 minute. Add the asparagus and stir over heat until their color turns bright and they are just tender. Remove from heat and add the soy sauce, vinegar, and sesame seeds. Serve warm or cold.

Serves 4 to 6.

NUT BUTTER COOKIES

We adapted this recipe from a '70's cookbook and it is timeless, easy, and foolproof. You can make these cookies with any sort of nut available and you won't find one that isn't fabulous. They are easy to throw together and the dough will keep in a wrapped log in the refrigerator for several days. *Note:* some nuts, particularly walnuts and pecans, will grind more easily if they are toasted for about 8 minutes at 325° and cooled before grinding. Gently toast any nut you use for more depth of flavor.

2 sticks (½ pound) butter
½ cup sugar
2¼ cups all-purpose flour
1 cup finely ground nuts (pistachios, almonds, pecans,
    or walnuts)
½ teaspoon vanilla extract

Preheat the oven to 375°. Lightly grease two cookie sheets. Set aside. In a mixing bowl, cream the butter until fluffy. Add the sugar and beat well. Stir in the flour, nuts, and vanilla at low speed. Roll into 1½-inch balls (or 2-inch balls for large cookies) and place about 2 inches apart on prepared cookie sheets. Press dough down to a thickness of ½ -inch with a fork or use the bottom of a drinking glass dipped in flour. Bake 10 to 12 minutes, until the edges are golden brown.

If you make the dough ahead of time, take it out of the refrigerator and bring it to room temperature before use. This makes it easier to work with and improves the cookies' texture.

Makes 20 medium cookies or 8 to 10 large.

BRUNCH FOR 8

CORN PANCAKES WITH SHRIMP PICO DE GALLO

GRANOLA

FRESH FRUIT WITH HONEY AND LIME

I like to let guests graze on fruit and granola while I cook the pancakes. They're wonderful right off the griddle and as long as they
are cooking, you'll have company in the kitchen. Black Pepper
Brownies (page 55) round out this menu if you want to offer a
sweet.

CORN PANCAKES

These pancakes may be made smaller for cocktail buffets. Though they're best eaten right away, they may also be made ahead and reheated. Top with the Shrimp Pico de Gallo or other salsas and cheeses.

3 ears fresh corn, stripped of silks, rinsed, and kernels
    cut from cobs
3 large eggs
1 cup milk
½ cup all-purpose flour
½ cup blue or yellow cornmeal
½ teaspoon baking powder
½ teaspoon kosher salt
2 whole green onions, chopped fine
¾ cup grated Monterey Jack cheese
cooking spray for griddle
sour cream for garnish, about 1 pint

Setting aside 1 cup of corn, combine the rest of the ingredients in a blender. Pulse until well mixed. Pour the batter into a medium bowl and stir in the rest of the corn.

Heat a griddle or heavy skillet on medium high heat and prepare with non-stick cooking spray. Pour ¼ cup batter onto the griddle for each 4-inch pancake. Cook for about 2 minutes each side. Keep warm in a low oven, covered with a damp cloth.

Makes about 2 dozen 4-inch pancakes.

SHRIMP PICO DE GALLO

Pico de gallo has one of the freshest flavors around. Tossed with shrimp and avocado, it's a cocktail that's hard to beat. If your onions are strong, limes are extra juicy or tomatoes are huge, just adjust ingredients to your taste. Remember to use gloves to handle the serranos—the heat lingers.

3 pounds raw shrimp
1 large yellow or white onion, chopped
5 large tomatoes (or about 9 Roma tomatoes), cored
    and chopped
½ cup cilantro leaves, chopped
juice of 4 to 6 limes
2 or 3 serrano peppers, seeded and minced
3 medium avocados, cut into ½-inch pieces
kosher salt and fresh ground black pepper

Bring a large stockpot of water to a boil. Add the shrimp and cook until they change color and are opaque, about 2 minutes. Drain and cover with ice. Peel, clean, and chop into ½-inch pieces. Refrigerate.

Combine the onion, tomatoes, cilantro leaves, lime juice, and serranos. Toss gently. Just before serving, add the avocado pieces and shrimp. Season to taste, adding more lime juice if needed. Serve chilled with warm corn pancakes.

Serves 8.

GRANOLA

I have played with this recipe to make it a little more healthful—using oil instead of butter—but with butter it really is tastiest. This granola is terrific served with non-fat yogurt and fruit. Allow about a quart and a half of yogurt for 8 guests.

1 stick (¼ pound) salted butter
⅔ cup brown sugar
1 cup honey
1 teaspoon vanilla extract
1½ pounds rolled oats
1½ cups unsweetened coconut flakes
½ cup shelled pumpkin seeds
½ cup shelled sunflower seeds
1 cup sliced almonds

Preheat the oven to 325°. In a heavy saucepan, combine the butter, brown sugar, honey and vanilla. Stir over low heat until the sugar has dissolved.

Combine the oats, coconut, pumpkin seeds, sunflower seeds, and almonds in a large roasting pan. Pour the butter mixture over the top and mix well. Bake 25 to 35 minutes, stirring every 10 minutes, until golden brown. Cool completely and store in an airtight container.

FRESH FRUIT WITH HONEY AND LIME

I feel a little silly putting a fruit salad recipe in this book. I only include it to help with quantities and a shopping list. Add or substitute any local favorites (grapes, papaya, star fruit, citrus, etc.) as you like.

1 cantaloupe, peeled and seeded, cut into 1-inch pieces
½ honeydew melon, peeled and seeded, cut into 1-inch pieces
1 mango, peeled and cut into ½-inch pieces
1-2 pints fresh berries
2 tart apples, seeded and sliced
juice of one lime
¼ cup honey

Combine fruit in a large bowl and gently mix. In a small bowl, whisk together the lime juice and honey and add to the fruit. You can prepare the fruit ahead (except for the apples and other choices that would brown) and wrap each kind of fruit separately until right before serving.

Serves 8 to 10.

SPOON fOOD

GAZPACHO
VEGETABLE WILD RICE SOUP
CREAM OF FRESH TOMATO SOUP
CORN AND PEPPER SOUP
FRESH SPINACH SOUP
MUSHROOM-SHALLOT SOUP

The spoon offers comfort. No hard or pointy edges, the shape of a nest, a gentle slope for the softest food, the first utensil offered a baby.

Lilly & Co. customers would call ahead to reserve a bowl of the daily soup. Many visited us several days each week just for soup. Any of these soups would make a great dinner, especially with bread, cheese, fruit or salad, and wine.

GAZPACHO

I have to admit that I never went quite crazy for cold soups, but I love this bold gazpacho with good Italian bread.

6 Roma tomatoes, core removed
1 small yellow onion, peeled
1 bell pepper (red, yellow, orange or green), seeded
1 medium shallot, peeled
2 cucumbers, peeled and seeded, ends trimmed
1 zucchini, ends trimmed
4 cups (1 quart) tomato juice
¼ cup olive oil
3 tablespoons red wine vinegar
⅛ teaspoon cayenne pepper
2 teaspoons kosher salt
1 teaspoon dill
3 fresh basil leaves, chopped
juice of ½ lime or 1 teaspoon sugar if needed for balance
    of flavor

Cut vegetables into 1½-inch chunks. In a food processor, pulse vegetables with tomato juice in batches, taking care not to purée too fine (the vegetables should be chopped well, but not pulverized). In a large container, stir the batches of vegetables with the rest of the ingredients and adjust seasonings. Serve chilled.

Serves 8 to 12.

VEGETABLE WILD RICE SOUP

1¼ cups uncooked wild rice
2 tablespoons butter
2 cloves garlic, minced
1 small yellow onion, chopped
½ cup chopped celery
2 carrots, chopped
2 ears corn, kernels stripped off of the cob
½ pound mushrooms, chopped
1½ cups chopped new potatoes (about 4 small)
8 cups chicken stock
kosher salt and fresh ground black pepper

For the garnish:
12 ounces fresh spinach, washed well and sliced thin
¾ cup grated Parmesan or Romano cheese

Rinse the wild rice and combine with 3 cups of water in a medium saucepan. Bring to a boil. Reduce to a simmer and cook for about 25 minutes, until the rice is just tender to the taste. Drain and set aside.

Meanwhile, in a stockpot, melt the butter over medium heat. Add the garlic, onion, celery, carrots, and corn. Cook until the vegetables start to soften. Add the mushrooms, new potatoes, and chicken stock and increase the heat to a simmer. When the potatoes are tender, add the salt, pepper, and the wild rice. Garnish each bowl with the spinach and cheese.

Serves 6 to 8.

CREAM OF FRESH TOMATO SOUP

This soup is a favorite, the little black skirt in the Lilly wardrobe (it goes with almost anything). I like it with a grilled cheese cooked in garlic butter; some employees wouldn't think of eating this soup without sinking a boiled egg into it. You can dress it up with croutons or chopped herbs if you like.

2 tablespoons butter
1 large yellow onion, chopped
3 cloves garlic, minced
2 medium russet potatoes, peeled and sliced
¼ cup tomato paste
2 pounds ripe tomatoes, quartered
kosher salt and fresh ground black pepper to taste
1½ cups half-and-half (or a mixture of equal parts cream and milk)

In a medium stockpot, melt the butter over medium heat. Add the onion and garlic and sauté until translucent. Add the potatoes, tomato paste, tomatoes, and just enough water to cover the vegetables. Simmer until the potatoes are cooked through. Purée until smooth in small batches, covering the lid of the blender with a kitchen towel to protect against splashes of hot liquid. Stir in salt, pepper, and half-and-half.

Serves 8 to 10.

CORN AND PEPPER SOUP

My sister arrived home one evening and threw together mostly canned items to make this soup. She claimed that it was delicious. Fresh is even better.

3 tablespoons butter
2 large onions, chopped
5 ears corn, kernels stripped off of the cob
2 red bell peppers, roasted and peeled (see note page 9)
2 poblano peppers, roasted and peeled
3 russet potatoes, peeled and cubed
2 cups half-and-half (or a mixture of equal parts cream and milk)
kosher salt and white pepper to taste

In a stockpot, melt the butter over medium heat. Add the onions and sauté until soft. Add the corn, bell peppers, and poblano peppers and stir for about 1 minute. Add the potatoes and enough water to cover and simmer until the potatoes are done, about 20 minutes.

Purée the soup in small batches until smooth, covering the blender lid with a kitchen towel to protect against splashes of hot liquid. Add the half-and-half and season to taste. The soup will thicken as it sits. May be served hot or cold.

Serves 12 to 14.

FRESH SPINACH SOUP

Perky green, this soup is simple, healthful and tasty. *Note:* save yourself the aggravation of having to fish the nutmeg chunk out of your fresh hot soup by grating it over a piece of waxed paper—not the pot—and sweeping the fragrant dust into the soup.

3 tablespoons butter
2 medium onions, chopped
2 small russet potatoes, peeled and sliced
8 cups chicken stock
1½ pounds fresh spinach, trimmed of stems and washed well
¾ cup sour cream
½ teaspoon freshly grated nutmeg
kosher salt and pepper
lemon wheels for garnish

In a stockpot over medium heat, melt the butter. Add the onions and sauté until soft. Add the potatoes and stock and simmer until the potatoes are cooked through. Remove from heat. While the stock mixture is still hot, stir in the spinach and sour cream. Purée the soup in small batches in the blender until very smooth. The soup should not be thick. This is a delicate purée; add more stock if the texture is not silky smooth. Season to taste. Heat the soup very gently and carefully after the spinach is added, else the color will turn drab.

Serves 8 to 10.

MUSHROOM-SHALLOT SOUP

This soup is a monochromatic brown, but the flavor is wonderful and anything but one-dimensional.

3 tablespoons butter
4 cups sliced shallots
4 cups roughly chopped mushrooms
8 cups chicken stock (more if necessary)
¾ cup raw rice (white or Texmati)
kosher salt and fresh ground black pepper
½ teaspoon fresh grated nutmeg
1 cup sour cream for garnish

In a stockpot over medium heat, melt the butter. Add the shallots and sauté for about two minutes. Add the mushrooms and cook for another 5 minutes. Add the chicken stock and rice and simmer until the rice is tender, about 12 to 15 minutes. Remove from heat and purée in small batches until very smooth (carefully, as always, with hot liquid—I cover the blender lid with a dish towel). The consistency should be somewhat thin, as the soup will thicken considerably as it sits. Add more stock if necessary and season to taste. Remember my advice about grating the nutmeg (see note, previous recipe); you will never find the whole spice if you drop it in this brown soup.

Serves 8 to 10.

INDEX

111